Opportunity In Disguise

How I Defeated Adversity

Revised and Updated

Marc Hoberman

LeRue Press, LLC

www.lrpnv.com

Order additional copies from:
LeRue Press, LLC
280 Greg Street, Suite 10
Reno, NV 89502
www.lrpnv.com
Bulk purchases and school discounts available.

Cover design by LeRue Press

First published in 2016 as *Search and Seizure: Overcoming Illness and Adversity*
Other Editions: Adversity Defeated
Revised and updated 2020-2021

ISBN 978-1-938814-33-4
Library of Congress Control Number: 2020951808

Praise for *Opportunity in Disguise:*
How I Defeated Adversity

"Whenever a great author pens a book, the impact of those words can influence millions. Marc Hoberman's book and words will inspire positive change in the lives of others for years to come."

Eugene Napoleon,
CEO of Nap Vision Entertainment, LLC.

"I have known Marc Hoberman as a brilliant speaker and student advocate, but I never knew that he also deals with epilepsy. This book was a revelation in learning how to out-create whatever struggles we are given, and turn them into gifts. I particularly loved reading his mother's advice after his first major epileptic episode:

> *"About an hour later, my mother came into my room and asked me to sit down. She told me that I was a handsome, musically talented, humorous young man who was given a gift by God. One of those "gifts" would now be my epilepsy. She said that it would keep me grounded and I needed to make it a strength, as opposed to a weakness, or crutch. Years later, I now realize that such words of wisdom should not have been taken lightly.*

Thank you, Marc, for your inspiration. Your Mom was a wise woman... and she raised an amazing son."

Barbara Niven-Actress,
Producer, Speaker, Media Trainer

"Plucking a book from the shelves with a well-written title, and not having a clue as what to expect, was rather surprising. Twenty-seven hundred and eighty-four miles, and a chasm between cultures divided Marc Hoberman and myself, however within a few pages he manages to skillfully breach that enormous gap.

While I had a mostly uneventful upbringing, Marc had the terrible misfortune of never knowing when a seizure would attack his body. The clock was always ticking in the background. Would he be embarrassed in front of his friends? Should he tell those close to him that he had this condition? What a terrible curse to have every waking moment of your life.

The mark of a good man is how he handles adversity. Marc not only conquered his malady, but he assisted others in understanding how a hardship can be overcome.

Hats off to Marc for an excellent and informative narrative."

Douglas B. Ashby, former
Los Angeles County Battalion Chief
and author of Heroes and Giants

"Once in a blue moon we find a literary piece that carries a powerful message to readers of all ages. Here it is—a work that can be treasured for the 'content of its character.

John McCormack,
award-winning author of
Jamaal's Journey

DEDICATION

To my wife, Ivy, who continues to be my source of strength.
To Craig and Scott, my sons, who keep me grounded and help me
realize what my priorities in life should be.
In loving memory of Sandra and Lee Hoberman.
Cathy Stiller = Strength.

In loving memory of
Andy "Big A" Lennane, "Later!"

ACKNOWLEDGMENTS

A special thank-you to my colleagues and friends, Susan Lorusso and Lori Stiller, whose invaluable editing skills and suggestions helped me see my story through the eyes of others.

A "shout out" to family friend Jack Mallia who gave me the feedback I needed from a teenager's point of view. Heartfelt thanks to my main editor, Jacob Hoye.

I also wish to thank my students, whose human frailties have given me the courage to share my personal story with others. My eternal gratitude to Janice Hermsen of LeRue Press and my publicist Bea Davis from Sassy B. Worldwide Productions.

TABLE OF CONTENTS

INTRODUCTION

The things in life that help us become successful and fulfilled can be based upon both positive and negative experiences. Our friends, family, colleagues, and personal decisions all assist us in becoming the people we see in the mirror each morning. In my case, a seizure disorder has taken me on many journeys in the past 35 years. These sojourns have allowed me to delve deeply into my soul and understand the many facets of my moral fiber and the character of those with whom I choose to surround myself. Some may see my illness as a weakness; however, I view it as an incredible strength and opportunity to educate myself and others. I have disclosed my infirmity to fewer than 10 people since I was first diagnosed over 35 years ago. The search for my identity has ended, and, just begun. I believe that I have now initiated the process to seize each and every opportunity not in spite of my illness, but because of it. As an educator, I am always struggling to think of new ways to impart knowledge to others. I wrote this book to remind myself and others of the importance of self-worth and inner strength. It is my hope that readers find strength, humor, and inspiration while reading *Opportunity in Disguise.*

Chapter 1

Embrace the Enemy

The enemy arrives without warning. The invisible, silent invader doesn't ask permission. It enters your brain quietly, suddenly and seizes control of everything, leaving you helpless in its grip. It takes possession and angrily throttles you, unleashing its rage on you. As if hypnotized into a stupor, you are dazed, unresponsive. You cannot refuse it. You can muster no resistance. You are turned off while it takes over—your own personal earthquake.

The quake bubbles up at full force as the powerful jolts and convulsions hurl you to the floor. When you return, you feel the pain of it all, see the terrible bruises and taste the blood in your mouth. Your tongue will be swollen, possibly gashed from your gnashing teeth. You might chip a tooth or break an arm. You might smash your head so hard on the concrete that you have a headache for days. You won't know what actually happened. You have no memory. The blessing and the curse. You'll ask and someone will describe for you how you looked like you were being tossed around as if in an exorcism, as if possessed by a terrible demon bent on destroying you.

An epileptic seizure is a powerful, remorseless enemy and it takes more than a bottle of pills to defeat it. You must search for a way to battle this invisible monster and decide to conquer the illness one day at a time.

Chapter 2

BACKGROUND CHECK

For as long as I can remember, I have been enamored of celebrities. Whether they are movie stars, television stars, or legends of the baseball diamond, I've always loved reading about people who live in the limelight. As a kid, I would mimic them in the mirror, act out my own real-life scenarios and vignettes, and give my own acceptance speeches at award ceremonies. My sister, Gayle, witnessed some of these speeches and has always enjoyed reminding me in front of others at family functions, however, you can't fight the truth, and those who know me are more than familiar with this obsession. Even now, my home office is replete with celebrity photos I have collected over the years. My favorites are the ones in which I am standing next to the likes of Denzel Washington, Mike Tyson, and, one of my idols, jazz trumpet legend Maynard Ferguson. A personalized autograph from Al Pacino sits atop one of my shelves. Stalking has its rewards.

Much of this obsession stems from my brief, life-altering meeting with the one major celebrity in our family, my grandfather, Harry Lubin. My mother's father was a highly successful television and film composer from the early 1940s through the late 1960s, who specialized in creating eerie, beautiful music, as he did for some episodes of *The Outer Limits, One Step Beyond,* and *The Loretta Young Show.* Even today, some of his music is used in a variety of episodes of *SpongeBob SquarePants.* He understood well what tone and mood was required for a given scene and prided himself on writing the perfect score, no matter the assignment. He was a mythic figure to me, even if he wasn't the greatest family man. He's likely the reason I got so into music and tried so hard to be a trumpet player. Some things just flow through the family. Some things are a gift and some are a curse. Still others are a little of both.

I only had the pleasure of spending time with my grandfather twice. Once when he flew in from California to visit my mother in the hospital after she'd suffered a stroke and again a month later when she left the hospital. I was just 11 years old. From this moment on, my family would have a long and arduous relationship with hospitals. And for much of that relationship, I would be the patient.

But on this day, hanging out with my famous Grandpa, things weren't complicated at all. And despite my mother's stroke and stay in the hospital, I was sort of blissfully unaware of the frailty of life and happy to be in the presence of the man I'd only heard stories about. If Harry Lubin were alive today, my students would say that he was "livin' large" and "all about dat life!" He wore expensive three-piece suits, stayed in the swankiest hotels, and only ate in the finest restaurants. He loved when doormen would look at him admiringly and say, "Good evening, Mr. Lubin." When he came in for his first visit, he took my father and me out to Amerigo's, our favorite Italian restaurant. It was one of former mayor Ed Koch's favorites, too. Tremont Avenue in the Bronx was a much better neighborhood in 1972 than it is today, and until its closing several years ago, Amerigo's would host the Hoberman family regularly for close to 30 years.

My father, Lee Hoberman, was one of the fussiest eaters on the planet. All the hundreds of visits to the restaurant and he never once ordered anything other than veal parmigiana for himself and the rest of us. In fact, it was only 20 years later when I went with my closest friend, Alan, and his Italian wife, Franzina, that I saw someone order something different. Frannie ordered dinner like a mafia don. Until then, I had never seen Italian food ordered without a Jewish New York accent before. I thought after she ordered bruschetta that she was going to shoot the waiter in the kneecaps and bury him out back. I can't say any more about her now because she still has me a little frightened.

Harry Lubin was no slouch when it came to ordering a meal. He requested escargot and about six other items I was unable to pronounce. My father refused to try anything new, but I had a blast experimenting with all those new dishes. When the check came, my grandfather opened his wallet and about 15 credit cards fanned out. Credit cards in 1972 were an anomaly. He gave me an expired one and I quickly added it to my collection of artifacts used to create the aura of being rich and famous. His brother, Ruby, was in town at the time, and we all met the next day. This was the only time that I met Uncle Ruby, but my connection to him runs deeper than any family gathering could ever accomplish. Uncle Ruby was an epileptic, and since it is often a genetic illness that usually skips a generation, it is most likely from him that I inherited the condition.

When my mother arrived home from the hospital about a month later, I went to spend the night with my grandfather in Manhattan at the exclusive Regency Hotel. It just so happened that he was in town on a business trip and invited me to spend some more time with him. I couldn't wait to inspect every little detail of his life, to see what I could glean about the way people in showbiz lived. The first thing I did when we entered the suite was open the closet. There were over 20 suits, each with its own matching Parker T-Ball Jotter pen clipped into the front pocket of each jacket. Parker T-Ball Jotter pens were the pinnacle of ballpoint pens and a must-have accessory, each one silver topped with a metallic colored lower half. He also had over 10 pairs of shoes. One would never know that he was in town for little more than a week. He had multiple options for whatever he wanted to do.

That night, we watched a movie together. He was lying sideways on the plush hotel carpeting doing leg lifts, explaining to me how the music did not match the action in the film and how the composer failed to achieve the correct mood. He was close to 70 then, but his physique was that of a man 20 years younger. It was clear to me that not only was he a man of great taste and style, he was a perfectionist, and I didn't doubt him for a second.

When we went down to breakfast the next morning, he ordered for me. Steak at 9 a.m. would not have been my first choice, but I was too busy paying attention to the plethora of employees greeting him with the "Good morning, Mr. Lubin," of which we had both become so fond. To me, it seemed the greatest thing in the world for people to know your name and I couldn't imagine a better feeling than strangers greeting you first thing in the morning.

He was wearing a beautiful sapphire and diamond ring that I stared at throughout the meal. He removed it from his finger, lifted up my hand, and placed it on my pinky.

"It doesn't fit now," he said, "but someday it will be yours."

That was the last time I saw him. He had invited me to California to visit him a year or two later, but that trip never happened. When I was 15, he was in a car accident near his home in Beverly Hills. The doctors said that were it not for him driving in a Cadillac, he would have died instantly from the impact. A few weeks later he suffered a major stroke that the doctors attributed to the accident, and he died shortly thereafter in the hospital. My mother and her sister, Terri, flew out to be with him and were able to spend a few days with him before he passed away. About four months later, a package arrived from California with the sapphire and diamond ring. I put it on my pinky. It fit perfectly.

In retrospect, I often feel as if I were cheated by not having more time with my grandfather. Our love of music was certainly one of the ties that bind, but I wish I had learned more about his extended family. In recent years, I have seen reruns on television that featured his music. It is almost surreal to think that he composed some of that music over 60 years ago. The emotions that touched my life decades after having met him run deep indeed. At a time when I kept my pain and emotional suffering inside, I wonder if he would have been someone I could have turned to for support and guidance. Sometimes, those you live with are too emotionally involved to give you the advice and guidance you need.

Perhaps his life experience and struggles could have been helpful to me in my time of need. In later years, I began to find books that spoke highly of his talents, and it was bittersweet that I found out more positive things about my grandfather from strangers than from him. As a child, it was difficult to access any of his music, Now, turning to my Amazon Echo and saying, "Alexa, play music by Harry Lubin," yields a myriad of beautiful songs penned by Harry Lubin. Perhaps my diagnosis could have brought us closer together. While I am blessed to have had such an incredible musician in my family, it is unfortunate that he wasn't actually in my life.

Chapter 3

Test Fail

Soon after meeting my grandfather, I would walk proudly around the house donning a sport jacket pretending to be my father, who owned a used furniture store. I would pretend I was buying used furniture for his antique business. The other half of my time was spent impersonating my grandfather closing music deals with major studios on musical compositions I had written. As a creative youngster, my stories and various scenes truly had no limits. Unfortunately, my celebrity ensemble was incomplete because I was missing the Parker T-Ball Jotter that I wanted to place in the inside pocket of the sports coat. These pens were $3 each, no small sum back then. I started taking cash out of my father's pants pocket each day in order to support my habit and went down to Max's Candy Store to get a nice new one, each one a different color from the last. There must have been an array of 50 colors, and I wanted all of them. Alan and I even went so far as to steal money from our friend Stuart, so Alan and I could buy more pens. Another student ratted us out after we bought his pens. His father grilled him about the $10 he came home with one day. The money was from our stolen pen fund and the kid couldn't take the pressure—he sang like a bird. The parent called the principal, and it all went downhill from there. Luckily, Mrs. Vitulli, the regular principal, was on leave for a few months. If she were in school, Alan and I would both be getting out of prison about now. Luckily, Mrs. Peace, the interim acting principal, was much more lenient. Of course, when my father found out, he was not as understanding as Mrs. Peace. In fact, he was about as lenient as Sonny Corleone was after his father, Don Vito, was shot. My father was old school, and when I admitted to taking money from him, he instructed my sister to get one of the belts from his closet. I don't know how she did it, but Gayle somehow found a homemade belt that must have previously been used as a torture device during medieval times. This belt had buckles on the buckles and little silver dots along the leather. He hit me with it a few times and, although it didn't hurt as much as I made it seem, my crying prompted my mother to step in and stop him. Scientific evidence may disagree, but I believe in the old adage, "Spare the rod and spoil the child." Most of my friends were hit as kids, and they turned out fine. I just wish my father had used a *rod* instead of that belt. It belonged in the Smithsonian, not a closet.

I tend to think that these thefts and other youthful indiscretions were a reaction to my mother's illness. She was hospitalized for close to a month after her stroke, and I had never spent more than a day away from her previously. On my father's behalf, it is rare indeed for a Jewish man to be without his wife for that time period and still be able to care for himself, let alone two children.

After about a week, he was able to secure help from his mother, Freda, who was known to me since birth as Bubbie, which is Yiddish for grandmother. I would never be happy that my mother was away, but I had always been crazy about Bubbie. Her cooking and baking skills were without equal. Oatmeal, homemade rugelach, and more adorned our kitchen table all day long. She babysat for us after school, helped my father with the laundry, and cleaned up after all of us. This was no simple task, since she was close to 80 years old at the time.

The only complaint Bubbie ever had pertained to our family dog. Pepper would take a crap almost daily right under the piano. I thought this was rather thoughtful of him since you did not have to hunt for his repulsive droppings around the house. Once when Alan slept over, he slid on Pepper's misplaced poop in the middle of my bedroom hallway. Surprisingly, Alan just wiped his feet with a tissue and went straight back to bed. He will deny this, of course, but my memories, as well as my olfactory senses, are quite vivid and accurate.

Pepper was not the best-behaved dog. He would steal roast chickens right out of the oven while my mother was on the phone telling a friend about her most recent purchases at Gimbel's. The Gimbel's Shopping Center was one of her favorite places to go. As a small child, I often went to Gimbel's with her and spent my time trying to arrange dates with the mannequins as she disappeared into the changing rooms to try on clothes. I'd walk up to a mannequin and say, "Meet me at Nathan's at 6." I would then proceed to the next one and say, "Meet me at Yonkers Bowl at 7:30." I was never once turned down for any of these dates, although, I was stood up a lot.

We paid $250 to have Pepper trained, since he always barked and never followed our commands to heal or do anything else for that matter. Although my wife thinks he was ugly, he was an adorable animal, but no trainer could match wits with him. When I had to put him to sleep 12 years later, my heart was broken. He was the first and only pet I ever had until I became a husband and father. I am amazed at how attached you can get to animals. My mother missed Pepper most of all. When I left for college at SUNY Albany, he was her primary companion. My father worked long hours each day and she spent most of her alone time with him. He accompanied us everywhere and was truly a part of the family.

Sadore Lane was an incredible place to grow up. Every aspect of our schooling and social life was centered around the unique five-building complex that I called home for the first 16 years of my life. My sister, Gayle, three years older, was born in Mount Vernon in 1959 where my parents lived when they were first married. My father told me that Sadore Lane was offering six months free rent, which he termed concession, when he first moved in. Real estate has certainly changed a lot since then.

I went to P.S. 31, which was about a 20-minute walk from my house. When it rained, someone's parent would drive us, but on most days a bunch of us just walked along together. It was easy for me to walk across the street since my overprotective sister dragged me by the collar at each crossing. She believed she was being my protector. I think there is a fine line between protector and executioner, but that is simply semantics.

By the time I was in sixth grade, we started attending what was then termed "boy-girl" parties. These consisted of cake, presents, and our new found interest . . . making out. We played the usual games of spin the bottle, post office, seven minutes in heaven, and many more. It was loads of fun except for the time when Darci refused to kiss me when my bottle spin landed on her just because I had braces. She said she was afraid that I might cut her lip. Nevertheless, this was a great time for me and my friends, but my fun would be interrupted abruptly one May afternoon.

I was about 12 years old when I thought I forgot my lunch money and decided to walk home from school with my friend Robbie to eat lunch at home. Robbie's father was a doctor, which was lucky for my family since after the events of that day, Robbie's dad asked him to explain exactly what had happened that afternoon. I was never able to answer those questions myself because I had no memory of what had transpired. I was incoherent during the walk home and simply followed Robbie. We both lived in Building Four. He lived on one side of the building, and I lived on the other. When I got to our apartment door, my mother was surprised to see me, since I was supposed to eat in school that day. I mumbled some excuse, and she gave me 50 cents to go to the milk machine in the basement. Next to the milk machine was a cigarette machine where my father would often buy a pack of Lucky Strike for 50 cents. When I failed to return after 15 minutes, my mother began to worry. She went downstairs to see what was taking so long and found me in the laundry room in front of the milk machine passed out and bleeding from the top of my head. Unable to pick me up by herself, she yelled for help, and a neighbor, Mr. Chester, came running. Mr. Chester was the grandfather of Dana and Denise Rogers. Their dad, a Sean Connery look-alike, was a poker buddy of my father's. Although Mr. Chester was no youngster, he was a tall, strong man and more than able to help my mother get me to the elevator and back upstairs and into my bed.

My mother called my father at work, and he came home immediately to take me to the hospital. My mother did not drive. My dad owned *Lee's Furniture*. He sold antiques and all types of used furniture for well over 20 years. It was a successful business, and he used to take me to work sometimes. We would enter old New York City buildings and ride old doorknob type elevators to apartments that housed some beautiful used furniture. Sometimes he would let me polish up oak desks in his store, and when I was finished with that, I would sweep the display floor. Then I would get into his white Cadillac and my mother would get in the back seat while I pretended to be her Limousine driver. I would make believe I was driving her all over Manhattan. I "drove" her to the opera, Broadway shows, fine restaurants and even the airport. The day she called my father to take me to the hospital was one of the first times I had ever seen him even slightly rattled. Once, I heard him yell in pain when he stepped on an open safety pin in the bathroom. Aside from that, he rarely showed emotion and was never sick a day in his life when I was a child.

I was admitted to the hospital later that day and the

doctor requested that I stay a day or two for tests. Oddly enough, another one of my dad's close friends, Jerry, had a daughter in the hospital with appendicitis. Coincidentally, we were placed in rooms next to each other. His daughter, Barbara, was a friend and classmate of mine and we had known each other for years.

I was given a brain wave test with contrast. That means that the doctors shoot iodine into your bloodstream so that they can see the activity in your brain. Years later it was discovered that I was allergic to iodine, which is why, during the procedure, I did not react well to the testing. I became nauseous within seconds and almost threw up. That test yielded a negative response. The next test was a brain scan, which also failed to show any abnormalities.

The only test that indicated any abnormality was the EEG or electroencephalogram. This test was actually pleasant for me in a weird sort of way. They glued electrodes to my head and flashed lights in my face while they monitored my brain's responses. It was almost as if I were receiving a 30-minute head scratching. That was certainly a favorite pastime of mine as a child. My mother would often scratch my head as we watched television together. She had long nails and I, much like a puppy, would revel in a scratching session. My father also scratched my head when we watched television. He, however, was the scratcher from hell. For some reason, he did not realize that it was deeply unpleasant to be scratched in the exact same spot for 20 minutes. I had to move my head from time to time just to be sure he didn't poke a hole in it.

The person who was preparing me for the EEG almost

put me to sleep as she rubbed the glue into my head and attached the electrodes to a variety of areas on my scalp. It is usually better if you are sleep deprived before the test, which I was not. It was during this hospital stay that I first learned that my grandfather's brother, Ruby, was an epileptic. My EEG did reveal some abnormalities, but the doctors said that because I recently sustained a head injury, I should probably come back in about six months and retake the test. They did not rule out the fact that I might have fallen because I was sick and the high temperature in the laundry room may have caused me to faint. It was even suggested that someone might have hit me on the head. Much time passed after that episode, and I never had the desire or need to return for further testing. In fact, I would not need to take tests such as those again for almost four years.

CHAPTER 4

A STROKE OF BAD LUCK

Since Sadore Lane was the only home I'd ever known, I was devastated when my parents told me we would be moving to Florida. I had made many friends over the years, had a girlfriend, was on the verge of getting my license, and was quite accomplished in the school band. I and was heartbroken to be giving all that up.

My father and his partners had two successful furniture stores now, and targeted Florida as a great opportunity for a third. They all agreed that my father, 55 years old and the eldest of the three, was the ideal person to oversee the expansion. And since Bubbie and my aunts already lived in Florida as well, my father jumped at the opportunity to relocate.

When they told me that we would be leaving in three weeks, I was shocked. I was completely blindsided, incapable of dealing with it. Gayle refused to go and made plans to stay with Joy, her best friend, who lived across the street in Building Three. Gayle and Joy had always been competitive with each other both socially and academically. Whether it was boys or jobs, they always vied for the top spot. One time, they were counselors together at a local day camp. Gayle asked one of the eight-year-old campers, "Who do you like better, me or Joy." Luckily for the camper, she chose my sister. I am pretty sure that little girl is now in therapy. Sadly, I didn't have the option to stay.

Sixteen is already a complicated age. When you tack on moving to a state 1400 miles away, you're only exacerbating an already tenuous situation. I was beginning my sophomore year of high school with friends I had known for over 10 years. Nothing I could say to my parents made any difference. By the time I was made aware, the move had already been set in motion. In no time at all, my parents had sold most of the furniture in the apartment as well as our recently acquired summer home in Torrington, Connecticut, and were packing us into the car for a 22-hour ride that would change our lives forever.

Some changes are easy to accept and others send shockwaves through your system and leave you feeling like you're hanging by a thread. Change had already been afoot in my life, but it was the kind you are grateful for when it happens.

After spending most of my life in an apartment, I loved our *summer home* in Connecticut. Torrington felt like an exclusive area, and, at the time, a popular racecar announcer, Brock Peters, lived there. There were two outdoor pools, three gyms, tennis courts, horseback riding stables, and even a garden was assigned to each semi-attached unit. Alan stayed with us for 17 days that first summer, lost 12 pounds and changed his hairstyle. Our house was like a celebrity rehab! My cousin, Candace, also stayed with us and went horseback riding with me. My horse was a bit horny and sniffed hers. Her horse kicked up and my horse went flying; I was barely able to hold on. I was definitely skittish the next few times we went riding, so I requested a horse that was closer to being sent to the glue factory. For extra exercise, I chopped trees in the backyard with an ax my father bought. This was my first experience with country living, or non-city living anyway, and I was sad to be giving it up as well as the relationships with friends and teachers that I had cultivated in New York over the years.

As we crossed the state line from Georgia into Florida, I took out my tape recorder and began interviewing my mother, who was in the front seat, about our journey and the move and life in general. I asked her what she was going to miss most in New York.

"I am going to miss Vandella," she said, "but I am going to LOVE Florida."

This 48-hour trip would prove to be the foundation for a much longer journey. It would prove to be a two-year experience that would shape my future and be the springboard that would mold me into the person I am today. Although four decades would pass from the day she made that statement, those few teen years and experienced that followed would prove to be beneficial to me and those whose lives I touched along the way.

Vandella was our cleaning woman and an incredible worker. She was so thorough that she wiped down my pen collection when she cleaned my room. Like most young boys, much of my childhood was spent with my finger in my nose. Vandella found the remnants of my nostrils under one of my shelves where I often placed them. My mother told her to complain to me directly. The second I came home from school my mother told me that Vandella had something important to say to me. I walked in my room and she said, "Marc, you know I love you and your family, but you have to start using tissues and stop picking your nose. Look at this rag. I cleaned up over 150 boogers!" A mortifying experience to say the least.

My mother's prediction was half accurate: she would miss Vandella, but she would not love Florida.

My mother was a special, singular woman. Her parents divorced when she was young. She and her sister, Terri, were brought up in a single parent family at a time when divorces were uncommon and a kind of stigma. She married my father when she was 26 years old and he was 34. They had a strong union forged from both happiness and struggle. My mother was instrumental in my father's business and both were generous in dealing with friends and family in times of need. Throughout everything, they maintained wonderful senses of humor. I never once heard my father or mother tell a traditional joke, but they taught me the importance of laughter in life and what an integral part it must play in all that we do. I remember when they went to have my sister fitted for braces. There was a glass display case on the wall of orthodontist's office containing over 40 molds of crooked and straightened teeth—before and after molds. My father started laughing and told my mother that it reminded him of a shoe store. She could not contain her laughter and her reaction made my father start *bounce laughing.* Everyone in the waiting room stared at them. The orthodontist got annoyed, came in and kicked them out for the duration of Gayle's visit, claiming that this was no laughing matter. My father straightened up quickly when he received the bill.

All our happiness and strength was tested sorely when, five years earlier, my mother was at a card game playing gin rummy with her friends. My father was at a poker game with his own friends that night. My parents were each excellent card players and loved to spend leisure time with friends throwing chips in an ever-growing pot. My father got a call that my mother had seemed to lose strength in her right hand and was slurring her speech. Luckily, one of the players in my father's game, Dr. Serating, was our family physician. He knew something serious was happening and called for an ambulance. My mother was rushed to Montefiore Hospital. The next day, my father made my sister and me breakfast and told us that my mother was not feeling well and had to spend another night at the hospital so that the doctors could give her some medication and make her feel better. My sister was 14. I was 10.

CHAPTER 5

TRUE GRIT

Isadore Lane was such that nothing stayed a secret for long.

"How is your mother?" a girl asked me in the school cafeteria the next day.

The girl standing next to me thought she was speaking to her.

"She is fine, thanks," she said.

"I was talking to Marc. Don't you know that his mother had a stroke last night?"

I didn't even know what a stroke was. I just said that she was fine and would be home later. I had no idea that *later* meant over a month. This would prove to be a most difficult time for my family, but because our friends and my grandmother rallied to our side, we were able to survive intact.

This was the event that brought my grandfather out from California. I can see now the seriousness of things that I was oblivious to then. As I said, this would be the first time I'd meet him. He and my father did not speak and my sister did not want to talk to him since she felt he had never attempted to know us. Harry's second wife,

Rose, made sure we each received a savings bond on our birthday, but our communication with him ended there. It was less a communication than a notification that he was out there somewhere and was a part of our lives, if only from a distance. I suppose if I were older I might have felt the same as my sister. My mother was shocked to see her father. I remember how she burst into tears when he walked in and embraced her. It must have been 12 years since they had seen each other.

I brought my mother a book of our family that I drew with crayons. It contained pictures of each of us, including Pepper. When she spoke, it was difficult to understand her because her mouth was slanted and her words slurred. My father visited her every day and my neighbor, Leatrice, would come by the apartment each night to pick out my school clothes for the next day until my grandmother came to stay with us. Leatrice's son, Howard, and I were good friends. When he first moved into the apartment complex, he had terrible asthma. He hacked louder than anyone or anything I'd ever heard. He and his sister were outstanding students and excelled in whatever they did. It is because of Howard that I decided to play the clarinet. I heard him practice one day and thought I would like to play the same instrument and hopefully play in the school band someday.

I only went to the hospital once while my mother was recovering and did not enjoy the visit. I was confused about her illness, and felt deeply uncomfortable around so much sickness and pain. I am hyper aware of any smells and aromas around me, especially unpleasant ones. This is a common condition of epileptics, this intense sensitivity to smell. The smell of the hospital gave me anxiety. I did not know then that I would be one of those patients in several hospitals only a few years later.

My mother finally returned home a month later in a wheelchair. I was stunned to see her rolling up the sidewalk. But as soon as she was at our door she stood up and refused to be wheeled into her own home. She used a cane instead, walked herself inside and immediately began to sob. She said she could not believe how beautiful my grandmother had kept the apartment. She walked into her room, opened the closet, and threw the cane inside. We never saw it again.

Although my father was the athlete in the family, my mother was a strong woman. She weighed over 180 pounds at the time of her stroke and was heavy most of her adult life. She was fond of telling us the story of her first date with my father, at which he told her over dinner that if she lost 10 pounds she would be perfect. She responded by telling him he could tear up her phone number. Luckily, he kept it. Her excess weight sometimes helped her, at least where I was concerned.

When I was in sixth grade, I took Judo lessons with my school friend Barbara's brother, David. His mother, Helene, drove us to the dojo twice a week. We often had to participate in a Judo drill where we had to push or pull our opponent out of a huge circle. The instructor, Kata Watanabe, a Judo champion from Japan, was an incredible sensei. He was also built like a brick house with teeth. One time I tried to push him out of the circle while he was standing on one leg. It would have been easier to move a building.

When it came to others my age, the matches in the circle were not as difficult, and I won most of them, but for some reason, I always lost at home when I practiced with my mother. She would not budge, and this was just a few months after the stroke.

She was a proud woman and did not care that her lower lip drooped slightly. She did exercises such as squeezing a ball and speech therapy to continue her rehabilitation. According to her doctors, she had recovered almost 95 percent from what should have been a debilitating blow. It was her inner strength along with my father's resolve that enabled me to deal with my own illness that was only three years away from rearing its ugly head.

CHAPTER 6

STINGING IN THE RAIN

By the time we arrived in Florida, I was extremely depressed. I didn't know anyone beyond my relatives, and was less than impressed with my classmates, many of whom were simply spoiled rich kids dedicated more to drugs than academics. I was never too keen on drugs. I started the semester six weeks behind schedule, which only exacerbated the problem. To top it off, the school system itself felt like a setback. The textbook they provided us for Advanced Spanish III was the same book I'd used the year before in Yonkers for Spanish II. Some of the teachers, too, seemed reluctant to push their students too hard. In my first math class we did absolutely nothing. The teacher literally said that because we were all so tired from being out so late celebrating the football team's victory the night before that she didn't want to begin a new unit. The football program seemed to be the school's top priority.

The school band doubled as the marching band and we rehearsed after school each day almost as long as the football players practiced. We had some excellent musicians, but I missed my band friends from New York terribly.

Back in junior high in Yonkers, I had overheard my band director playing a jazzed up version of the Rocky theme featuring a jazz trumpeter named Maynard Ferguson. I had never heard of him before, but instantly fell in love with his powerful screeching high notes. Thirty years later, and after seeing him perform more than 20 times, I was able to hire him for a fundraiser at Spring Valley High School where I was teaching at the time. Much to my surprise, when I first entered the Florida band room as a tenth grader, several trumpet players were rehearsing and playing some of Maynard's songs, and one kid in particular was matching those notes. I was excited that others shared my admiration for a professional musician, but it turned out that our respect for Maynard was all that we had in common. Nothing else developed in the way of friendship.

The football games were always at night, and the first one I attended was played under an ominous sky. While waiting in the parking lot to line up, the skies opened and it began to pour, a tropical downpour unlike anything I'd ever experienced. Hard, heavy rain that hurt as it hit you. I never felt so alone in my life. I barely knew anyone and just stood there getting drenched as band members got into cars to stay dry. It was the first time in my life that I felt truly alone. Finally, Larry, a clarinet player I had spoken to in class a few times, invited me into his family's car until the rain passed.

Around this time, we were waiting for our house to be built in Emerald Hills, an affluent community. We stayed in an efficiency hotel in the Hollywood area. Across the street was Swenson's Ice Cream Parlor where I got a job as a busboy and became friendly with another busboy who attended my school. Luckily, he and I shared the same lunch period, so I didn't have to eat alone. I had gone from eating with 15 friends back in Yonkers, to eating with just one.

I was anxiously awaiting the move from the hotel into our house in Emerald Hills. During the tour of the model home, my parents surprised me when they took me into the backyard and showed me the small yet beautiful swimming pool. Each night I dreamt of swimming in that pool. Moving from an apartment to a house with my own swimming pool would be quite a change. We would have been the only people in the neighborhood that weren't doctors or lawyers. My father had done well with the furniture business in New York, and he and my mother made a respectable profit on the summer home they sold.

The plan was to open the Florida location with furniture shipped from the two New York stores and continue the success that my father and his partners had enjoyed in New York City for the past 20 years. When I reflect on this part of my life, the words of Robert Burns come to mind: "The best-laid plans of mice and men often go awry." The combination of my medical condition and the poor location of Lee's Furniture South led to an early closing. We never moved into Emerald Hills, and although my father was no poet, I believe that an old saying he repeated described our situation best: "Man plans and God laughs." I, however, would fail to see the humor.

My cousin Marc was a year older than I was and was accepted to the University of Florida in Gainesville the following year. I missed him a lot since we had grown so close over my year there. We hung out all the time. He was immensely popular at the school and tried to introduce me to many people, but I did not have much in common with his friends. I became closer with his sister, Candace, or Candee as I called her, the year he went away. One weekend, he invited us to visit him at school. It was about a four-hour drive and we left at five a.m. so we would have an entire day of college partying.

The day before, I was testing out the wheel alignment on my car the way my father had taught me. I would let go of the wheel briefly and "ride the break" to see if the car would stay straight. The wheels were not aligned well, and the car swerved several times. I was only half surprised when I was pulled over by the police. The officer thought I was driving drunk, but when I told him why the car was swerving, he just told me to drive safely and have a nice trip.

That Saturday morning, we packed my 1977 red Ford Mustang and began our journey. I had bought the car shortly after we arrived in Florida with money I had saved up and a nice contribution from my father. On the road to Gainesville, we blasted Boz Scaggs on the Marantz stereo system that Marc had installed just a few weeks prior to his departure for college. Unfortunately, we never made it to Gainesville. In fact, we were barely on the road for 10 minutes before my life took a dramatic turn.

Most of that morning has never returned to my memory. I only know what Candee told me. At some point between getting on the highway and our first turn, I became incoherent. After passing our first exit, I recall Candee telling me that I had missed our exit. I turned around and we passed the exit again.

It was as if my mind and body were separating, at odds with each other. After the third attempt, we exited and approached the tollbooth. According to Candee, I let go of the steering wheel and my body tightened as I succumbed to the grip of my first seizure.

She grabbed the wheel and steered us through the tollbooth. As she could not reach the break, she threw the car into park. Immediately, a police car pulled up and an officer came to the window. I was barely conscious and somehow said I was fine. I got out of the car and immediately tipped over. Luckily, the officer caught me before I hit the pavement. He asked Candee if I was on drugs. She told him there was no way, that she had no idea what was happening. She was terrified.

An ambulance was called to transport me to the emergency room. I don't remember what happened there either. I only remember being released a few hours later and given a bottle of Dilantin, an anti-seizure medication.

My parents were at a flea market selling socks, shorts and shirts. This was the business venture my father settled on after the store in Florida failed. He semi-retired after selling off his share of the furniture business. I walked into the condominium with Candee and told my parents the story of what had happened.

When we are faced with adversity, the fight or flight response often takes over. Most adults don't realize how adverse conditions can actually help them learn to adapt and improve. For young people, teens in particular, it is nearly impossible to see the forest trees. Far too many people don't realize the strength of the human spirit. For me, this new diagnosis was a recipe for disaster. I was ill-equipped to deal with the reality that I was no longer in control of my brain and my body.

Between a last-minute move to another state and now this new sickness, I felt as if I had nowhere to turn. There was no proverbial cloud with a silver lining. I could never have imagined how I would learn from my struggles. My adversity would eventually transform itself into an opportunity. Throughout my years in education, I have seen students who were unable to focus on anything other than their troubles. By definition, wisdom and experience are developed over time. Of course, I didn't realize it then, but these problems were necessary for me to learn more about myself and understand how to grow despite life's obstacles.

This was only the beginning of a painful, arduous journey that would turn out to be the illness that has helped to change and shape my life. There were highs and many, many lows along the way, but it is certainly true that what doesn't kill us makes us stronger. It is also true that what makes you stronger sometimes nearly destroys you on the inside along the way.

CHAPTER 7

GROUNDED

My mother, a person who cried at anything emotional, including game shows and sentimental television commercials, seemed surprisingly calm when she came home and found out that I had been in the hospital for a few hours. She and my father went into the bedroom for a while. I could hear them talking, but was unable to make out what was being said. About an hour later, my mother came into my room and asked me to sit down. She told me that I was a handsome, musically talented, humorous young man who was given a gift by God. One of those "gifts" would now be my epilepsy. She said that it would keep me grounded and I needed to make it a strength, as opposed to a weakness, or crutch. Years later, I now realize that such words of wisdom should not have been taken lightly. However, at the age of 16, being unable to control when I might have a seizure, publicly or in private, did not make me feel gifted. Through the years, I have suffered with this illness, learned about it, and, from it. It is a major part of who I am because it is part of me.

As a youngster, I was rarely sick. Except for the occasional cold and fever, I hardly ever needed medication of any kind. I woke up the morning after my seizure, walked into the bathroom, and opened the medicine cabinet where the Dilantin was housed and was greeted by a small bottle with a two-week supply of pills. My parents were told to take me to a neurologist to help find the best medicine for me. Dilantin would help keep me seizure free for the time being. To this day, I do not believe I received the care needed to monitor my disorder, and I spent many months experimenting with a variety of prescribed drugs that did not help me in any way. The first visit to the doctor was depressing since I did not see myself as someone with an illness. There were many people in the waiting room and I did not want to be associated with sick children. I felt sorry for the young children I saw in the waiting room. Some had ticks, another was drooling, and some seemed to have no visible infirmities at all. I wondered if they looked at me as I looked at them—*What's wrong with him? What sickness does he have?*

After a subsequent visit, a doctor added a drug called Tegretol to the Dilantin I was taking. I was only 17 years old at the time, and soon learned that epilepsy is often hereditary. As I mentioned earlier, my grandfather's brother, Ruby, suffered from epilepsy as well. Supposedly, it skips a generation, but I am not sure if that has ever been medically proven. I was informed that I was not allowed to drive a car for at least six months, a terrible blow from which I was not certain I would recover. As a teenager with a license and a Mustang, I did not want to depend on others for transportation, and I felt truly disabled when I had to give my car keys to my father. I had to get a ride to school every day from a neighbor, and my father had to pick me up after school on days that I stayed for marching band.

The doctor wanted my teachers to know about my disorder but I refused to tell them. The band director called me into his office and said that my parents had called the school and alerted the nurse and the principal about my recent health issue. He asked how I felt and what he should do if I had a seizure. I was clueless as to how I should answer him. I was not really conscious or aware of anything during my seizures and had no idea what he should do if I had one in his presence. I told him the nurse would be better informed than I was. I was humiliated that my teachers would now be judging me differently, and I often wondered if each time they looked at me they were looking for warning signs of a seizure.

When I became a teacher years later, my close friend and colleague Lori Stiller, a health teacher in my school, had a student who was leaning on the wall near the window before class began. He had a seizure and almost fell out the window. Luckily, she teaches on the first floor. As it turns out, he was actually a runner on the cross-country track team which I was coaching that year. There was nothing in his records that indicated he suffered from seizures, and his parents said he never had an episode in the past. He wasn't allowed to practice with the team or participate in meets until several weeks later after being cleared by his doctor. He never had another seizure again, but I am not sure I ever looked at him the same way. I was always looking for him to exhibit signs of his next seizure. I often wonder how others, ignorant about epilepsy, reacted to my school medical cards when I was a teen. Were they always looking at me, frightened that I would have a seizure in their classroom? Was I treated differently? Pitied even? There needs to be more open discussion about illnesses that youngsters may have. This is for the benefit of all, not just the afflicted. Teachers, students, family, and friends alike should be more educated about the illnesses that are prevalent in the school community. If people are not informed, they often make snap judgments and generalizations that are hurtful to those suffering from the malady. With the advent of social media, more problems can be created which cause unwanted and harmful "side effects" above and beyond those experienced from the condition or medication. I like to think that my experiences have helped me develop a special sensitivity to my students who suffer from chronic illnesses. Having been in their shoes, I know how they feel.

CHAPTER 8

IT AIN'T SO GRAND

There are many types of seizures. As time passed, I researched epilepsy at the local library to learn more about my condition. This was, of course, prior to the Internet, and it took days to get information that would now be readily available to me in a matter of minutes. I looked to experts from the Mayo Clinic and other esteemed places for information that would educate me about the condition I would carry for the rest of my life.

A grand mal seizure, also known as a tonic-clonic seizure, is a common type of seizure characterized by loss of consciousness, falling down, loss of bowel or bladder control, and rhythmic convulsions. Seizures often result from an abnormal electrical discharge in the brain. Other types of seizures include petit mal seizures and temporal lobe seizures. Although the cause of seizures can vary, many times the cause is unknown while other times seizures run in families. Repeated brain seizures are what characterize people as having epilepsy. What I did not realize was that about 10 percent of Americans experience a single seizure episode during their lifetime. Only about three percent of these people will go on to develop epilepsy. More than two million Americans have epilepsy.

Although my seizures end with grand mal episodes, they begin with a petit mal seizure. This is also known as an absence seizure and most often occurs due to abnormal electrical discharge in the brain. Usually, a petit mal seizure involves a brief, sudden lapse of conscious activity. Each seizure may last minutes, but hundreds may occur each day. During a petit mal seizure, small jerking movements are sometimes seen in the muscles, jaw, or hands. A person who experiences a petit mal seizure can usually resume normal activities after the seizure ends. Before we found the best doctor for my condition, I suffered from both petit mal and grand mal seizures concurrently. My grand mal seizures were always preceded by petit mal seizures. As it turns out, this was helpful for my parents. My petit mal seizures lasted for hours and prepared us for the upcoming bigger, more intense, seizure. These are grand mal seizures but they are anything but "grand." During petit mal seizures, I would become increasingly incoherent. This included speaking gibberish and completely losing focus, something my doctor, years later, would term *absences*. Before my current medication was prescribed, I always had a grand mal seizure after the petit mal seizure. This is the seizure with which most people are familiar. I would almost always fall down, my body would jerk, and I would clench my teeth. There were several times when I sustained injuries including chipped teeth, a bloody tongue, and bruises.

There were certainly social implications as well. My

demeaner started to change as I carried the constant fear that I was unable to control my brain, and by extension, by body. The few people in my inner circle who knew about my diagnosis tried to be supportive, but I could tell that they were as mystified and frustrated as I was. This was not an illness that was well known, and a grand mal seizure in particular was a frightful thing to witness. For me, the combination of the social aspects of the disease as well as my own insecurities were devastating. This is an enemy you are unable to see, and it leaves you helpless, injured, embarrassed, and depressed.

CHAPTER 9

THREE STRIKES

Even as a youngster, I used my sense of humor to my advantage. I loved watching comedians on various television shows, and I was always in the middle of a new joke book. Luckily, I seemed to have an incredible memory and was able to recall hundreds of jokes. I was able to compartmentalize them into the various categories in which they belonged. As I got older, it became both a defense mechanism as well as a coping mechanism. I turned my sense of humor into a strategy. After my epilepsy diagnosis, I used my sense of humor to deflect the negative aspects of my illness. I even told some epilepsy jokes I had heard. While I was able to tell jokes to give the appearance that I was not depressed and even happy, that was not the case. Through the years, my sense of humor has enabled me to overcome much adversity, not just the issues I experienced due to my sickness.

As a teenager, my father was a great baseball player and very much wanted me to pick up where he'd left off. He had a tryout scheduled with the Yankees, but missed it when he enlisted in the army at the beginning of World

War II. It wasn't until I was an adult with children that I learned my father was able to leave the army early because he had volunteered for so many missions. He also confided in me that he was shot in the forearm while serving in New Guinea. I am always amazed how many World War II veterans never even mention their experiences in the armed services.

Although I was a fast runner and as wiry as he was, my performance on the baseball diamond was less than stellar. Before my cousin Marc left for college, he invited me to play in a game with his friends. It wasn't bad enough that I was not good at baseball; salt was added to the wound when I arrived to find all of Marc's jock friends ready to do serious battle. Sadly, I struck out all three times I came to the plate, on the minimum number of pitches no less.

All of the extended family members got together for a barbecue that evening. My father asked about the game and how I had done. Marc was all too eager to report on my failures at the plate.

My father turned to me.

"Why did you strike out three times?"

I had to be honest.

"Because I wasn't up four times!"

My family members laughed; my father, not so much.

CHAPTER 10

I SCREAM YOU SCREAM . . .

Epileptics struggle on many fronts, but there are two issues that are especially difficult to navigate.

The first is that there are often no warning signs that a seizure is about to occur. Your friends and family may realize one is about to occur after seeing you go through enough of them, but you rarely have any idea one is coming or already happening, The second is the wet blanket it throws over your entire life, especially as a teenager. You'd prefer to ignore the illness or make it adapt to your way of life. Sadly, the illness wants *you* to adapt and therein lies the struggle. The epilepsy and you are at war for your body.

After the seizure I suffered on the way to visit Marc, I was told that I would not be able to drive for several months. I would not be able to drive myself to school or work. This was a terrible blow given that I had always been independent. Although I would gladly do favors for family and friends, asking others for help did not come easily. Losing my car didn't do much for my romantic life either.

The first medication I was given was Dilantin. This was one of the most prevalent anti-seizure drugs prescribed in the 1970s. It was a powerful drug with numerous side effects. The one that bothered me the most was my gums swelling and bleeding. All day long I could taste blood in my mouth.

Most weekends I just stayed home. I didn't go out with friends as much as I had before. My friend, John, tried to intervene and told me to stop being so depressed, to get out and party. I met John at Jaxson's Ice Cream Parlor in Dania. Jaxson's was more popular and exciting than Swensen's. In fact, it was more of a landmark than an ice cream parlor. The ice cream was handmade on the premises, and going to Jaxson's was an event. The outdoor area was a virtual carnival, with cotton candy machines, a unicycle rider, and a candy store. Inside was a fantasy world with the best ice cream menu I have ever seen. The featured item, The Kitchen Sink, boasted more than 10 ice cream flavors and was served in a miniature kitchen sink. The largest dessert item, The Punch Bowl, consisted of over 20 flavors and a variety of toppings. The cost matched the year. When I started working there in 1979, the Punch Bowl was $19.79.

Jaxson's was owned by Monroe Udell and was truly a great place to eat. Monroe made the ice cream for over 40 years and only passed away recently. His daughter, a close friend of Candee's, now runs the business. It wasn't exactly the greatest place to work, but the eating experience was outstanding. Jaxson's is still around today with the same great menu. When I visited Florida in 2013, the Punch Bowl, which feeds 15 people, was $99.95.

I met some colorful characters at Jaxson's and became friendly with several of the staff. John was one of them. He was a great kid. At the age of 16, he was a man in a teen's body. He was from a much tougher neighborhood in New York than I was. His dad had been a soldier in Vietnam and suffered from terrible nightmares. He would howl in his sleep and flail around like he was fighting or dying or drowning. His mother forced him awake by poking him with a mop handle to help him escape the terror. John's father passed at an early age. His mother remarried and they all relocated to Florida around the same time I arrived.

One day John's girlfriend said she had a friend who wanted to double date and John asked me to come along. I was still having trouble with my medication and was not in the best of moods. I didn't know it then, but one of the reasons I was struggling so much with my mood was that the dosage of Dilantin I had been prescribed was too intense for my body. For one, it made me incredibly dizzy at night. I just assumed the dizziness was a side effect of the epilepsy and didn't want to burden my parents any further, so didn't tell them about it. I knew so little and assumed too much. I thought certain things were a result of the epilepsy that were actually the result of something else. The dizziness was so intense at night that I often had to crawl from the living room to my bedroom because I was unable to walk a straight line without falling or walking into the walls. Every night I waited for them to fall asleep before crawling to my room. Nevertheless, I agreed to join John and his girlfriend for the double date that evening.

We began the evening at *The Castle*, a great venue that featured bumper boats, miniature golf, and a giant arcade. A few hours into the evening, I felt the dizziness come on. It's almost like you've been drugged without knowing it. One minute you feel one way and another you feel sick, like you've been poisoned, like someone slipped something in your drink. I was able to get to the men's room before my date or John noticed. I barely made it to the stall before I threw up. I almost fainted and had to hold on to the toilet paper dispenser as I wretched uncontrollably into the toilet. Although I felt much better, I was in no mood to continue the date and had to ask them to take me home.

CHAPTER 11

The Fountain of My Youth

I had finally reached a tipping point with the dizziness. I broke down and told my parents and they took me back to my neurologist. He ordered blood tests, which revealed that the dose of Dilantin was toxic and the root of the problem. He subsequently lowered the dosage and I soon started feeling better in the evenings.

John was not the only interesting character at Jaxson's. It seemed that all the weirdos in the area worked there at one time or another. Larry and Jeff worked there a few months before I was hired and, despite their numerous warnings to me about the management, I applied for a job anyway. Every job has its whackos, and Jaxson's was no exception. To this day, my fond memories of eating myself into oblivion still pale in comparison to the experiences I had there.

The owner's nephew and manager, Joe, either loved you or hated you, depending upon the day of the week. When I started, I couldn't help but notice that several of the workers seemed to enjoy spraying their mouths full of whipped cream, but I never saw the cream in their mouths. Turns out they were doing whippits. I had no idea you could get high on the air inside the canister. They just loved starting their shifts on a HIGH note!

Larry and Jeff worked at the fountain, and I was a busboy. Throughout the night, I could have as many free shakes as I wanted. Although I gained over 10 pounds, aside from my time at college, this was the most fun I ever had getting fat.

Larry made the best shakes but didn't last too long at the job. Joe pinched his ass one night as Larry was cleaning the ice cream containers. Larry called him a "faggot." Joe asked him to repeat what he said and Larry replied, "I said I'll have these cans cleaned in 10 minutes." A few days later, Joe fired Larry for some ridiculous reason using his catchphrase; "I don't think we need you anymore." It's hard to explain how he sounded when he fired people with that infamous line each week, but it sounds a lot like Peter Lorre in any Bogart film.

I was one of the best busboys at Jaxson's. I was fast and efficient at clearing the tables. Although I was asked to move up to waiter on several occasions, I never wanted that responsibility and was more than happy earning $35 a night each weekend. This included my paltry salary as well as generous tips from the wait staff. This was an enormous amount of money for a 17-year-old in 1978.

While I was there, they hired a piano player for the weekends. Jaco was 27 years old, and about 235 pounds. He was close to six feet tall and carried his weight well. Although he had one of those round jolly faces that heavy people often possess, you could tell that in his younger years, he had been quite good looking. After we became close friends, he showed me a picture of him 10 years younger with long brown hair and a bevy of beauties surrounding him. He may have been an ice cream parlor piano man when I met him, but he was a hard rocker with enormous talent previously. He played me a few songs from a cassette that he recorded with his band a few years prior to us meeting. It was really good, and had he not had a string of really bad breaks, I think he could have done well in the industry. Jaco and I shared an infatuation for boxing and often watched matches on television together. He also boxed a bit when he was younger and he and I often sparred for kicks and to stay in shape. We also jammed together and even performed a command performance for my Aunt Bette and Uncle Bob at their condo. "Hava Nagila" and "When The Saints Go Marching In" were just some of the songs on our playlist that day. Jaco's wife got a job working at the fountain at Jaxson's a few weeks after he was hired and, as time went on, we all became quite close. They would soon become all too familiar with my seizures in a most unexpected place.

Regrettably, while at Jaxson's, I spent some parts of my breaks in the large storage refrigerator eating barbecued drumsticks that never made their way to the food and salad bar. I easily consumed four drumsticks a night and still have nightmares that I turn into a lump of poultry while standing on the North Pole.

After a few months, I was told that they were short on waiters, and I would have to accept a promotion. They said it would be a cinch since I was the best busboy in the restaurant. How wrong they were. The difference between being a busboy and a waiter is tantamount to the difference between the Yankees and the *Bad News Bears*. I was horrible. I never learned how to write down the orders properly and often forgot things as simple as bringing silverware to the table. This is not something you can simply apologize for at an ice cream parlor where desserts melt at an alarming rate onto the customers' clothing.

At first, the manager thought he gave me too many tables. His new strategy was to give me one table for the night until I became more adept at the job. All that did was reduce my horrible service to one table at a time instead of three. The third night as a waiter, I delivered a dish of ice cream to a table without the Jaxson's signature mini-parasol and Joe called me into the kitchen.

"Why is the dessert missing the parasol?" he asked? This was a signature decorative addition.

"I forgot," I told him.

"I don't think we need you anymore," he said as he turned and walked away.

Although I enjoyed my job at Jaxson's, I wasn't really disappointed that I was fired. Even as a young child, I was told that as long as I did my best, that would be fine with my parents. On the occasions when I failed math exams, if I did my homework and studied, my parents were not upset with failing grades. I was a fairly good student, and the level of expectation that my mother and father set for me always focused on effort, not simply results. I had a job since the age of 12 delivering the coupon magazine, The Pennysaver to residents in my building, and always had a babysitting job and worked for my father once in a while on weekends. I knew I would find another job soon, so I accepted my situation with a positive outlook and knew that no matter what, I could always count on me.

When I explained the situation to my parents, I did a really good impersonation of the manager, and that certainly lightened the mood. There was nothing better than free ice cream, and my stomach suffered more than my ego.

CHAPTER 12

GOOFY IN DISNEY

A few weeks after I left Jaxson's, Jaco and his wife asked me if I wanted to join them for a weekend at Disney World. I had a good amount of money saved and hadn't started a new job yet, so I said yes. It was about a four-hour drive and we told jokes and sang songs the entire ride. When we arrived in Kissimmee, just outside of Orlando, we stopped at an All You Can Eat Spaghetti Restaurant. After each plate we finished the southern waitress asked, "Y'all want a repeat?" She had to ask that 11 times as Jaco broke all records for the most pasta eaten by one man (or farm animal for that matter). I looked under the table to see if he was stuffing spaghetti into an extra wooden leg. We rolled out of there about two hours and 20 pounds later. Homer Simpson could not have eaten more.

When we got to the motel, I realized that I had forgotten to bring my medicine. Since we were only staying two nights, I wasn't too concerned. We got to the Magic Kingdom late the first night and only spent a few hours. Although it was my seventh time there, words can't describe the transformation that takes place as you enter Disney World. It truly is the most magical place on earth, and that night was no exception. There's nothing better than watching the flashing lights of the evening parade and eating cotton candy with friends. Somehow, we found room in our pasta-filled bellies to add jelly beans, hot pretzels, licorice and more. When we returned to the motel, we planned out the next day so we could do as much as possible before we left the following morning.

Although Jaco and his wife stayed, I never returned that day. I had a grand mal seizure in the motel room early the next morning. I have absolutely no memory of that episode. Jaco and his wife had to watch me for several hours until my parents arrived. According to them, I had one or two smaller seizures while they stayed with me. I also was incoherent for a few hours, but they didn't recognize that as the preface to the seizure to come. Jaco said he asked me a question about what I wanted to do that day and my reply was, "Yep, what time is it?" He didn't know if I was being funny or just tired from the night before. My cousin Marc drove my parents up to the motel in his Trans Am immediately after Jaco's frantic call to my parents' house. As it turned out, this was not the best vehicle in which to transport an epileptic. I was not totally conscious or aware of what was going on and kept trying to stand up in the car during the entire ride home. This was a difficult trip for my parents who had to spend eight hours in a car that was meant to be a chick magnet, not an ambulette. I was awake, but in no way cognizant any time during the car ride home. Although I missed two doses of medicine and that caused my seizures, I often had seizures, even while on the medication. This episode, coupled with missing my home in Yonkers, spun me into a depression from which I wasn't sure I would ever recover. To make matters worse, Alan had called and told me that back in Sadore Lane my father's friend, Jack, asked how I was feeling. When Alan said I was feeling fine, Jack said, "How can he be fine if he has epilepsy?" Up until this time I had no idea that any of my parents' friends knew about my condition. I was humiliated. These things weren't supposed to happen to young people, least of all me.

Alan was continuing his popularity and great high school experiences in Yonkers. He was planning for the prom with his girlfriend and his friends. Plans that included limousines and pictures were all things I should have been experiencing. Not to sound overly dramatic, but my heart truly ached. My friend Evelyn, who I met in band class in seventh grade, was constantly updating me about our high school band. She wrote about how they were learning to create a halftime show for our football games. The band members were incredibly close because we traveled together as a class from seventh to ninth grade. I received a letter from her that described our band director, Mr. Krell, walking behind the marching band as they simulated a rocket ship. Mr. Krell was at the end of the "ship" with a fire extinguisher, which, from the stands, looked as if it were blasting off. I remember reading the letter in my bed, tears flowing down my face. I felt as if I were robbed of my high school years, and I had to live those experiences vicariously through friends I had been standing next to just a year earlier.

My head was often spinning daily despite the new doses of medicines. I ruined my friend's Disney vacation and frightened my parents beyond measure. I saw no proverbial light at the end of the tunnel, and had to use my sense of humor as a defense mechanism so those around me would not know how much I was suffering on the inside. My parents' finances were not as strong as they had been in the past, and I did not want to burden them any further with my health issues.

A week after Disney, my father took me to the doctor's office to see if my medications could be changed yet again. About a half hour before the appointment I began to feel lethargic and was finding it difficult to focus while my father was speaking to me. Once we got into the office, I lost all memory of that visit. While being examined by the doctor, I had another seizure. My father didn't want me to bite my tongue as I had done during one of my other seizures, so he put his wallet in my mouth. I usually didn't remember anything after a seizure for at least a day or so. Two days after the seizure he took out his wallet and showed me the deep teeth indentations that I had left in the leather. There is a common misconception that epileptics are at risk of swallowing their tongues during an "episode." This is not the case, and the only reason my father used his wallet was to prevent me from biting my tongue. Based on the bite marks he showed me, I surely would have bitten a good part of my tongue off. I have bitten my tongue at least five times during various seizures and the pain that follows for the next few days is excruciating. Carrying around a wounded tongue in your mouth that's been crushed by your own merciless teeth is a torture I wouldn't wish on my worst enemy. It's similar to biting into your own lip while you're eating and then biting into it again and again. Imagine that and make it worse. Then you're getting close to what it feels like to bite your own tongue during a seizure.

I was going in and out of a state of depression almost daily. The only way I could think of to fight back was with knowledge. I contacted the Epilepsy Foundation as well as the Mayo Clinic and received many pamphlets about my illness. This was no small task for a 17 -year-old teenager, and I almost felt as if I were reading a work of fiction. I would imagine that I was doing research for a book report on epilepsy, but then reality set in; my reality. Learning more about my illness put me in a position to embrace my adversity or, at the very least, meet it halfway. I wasn't willing to let it control my entire life, but this philosophy did not take hold overnight. There were many setbacks along the way, but I started to become my best advocate. I went to the library and read sections of books about epilepsy and read over the pamphlets repeatedly. I may have become an epileptic overnight, but overcoming my adversity was a long, hard journey.

CHAPTER 13

RORER 714

We moved a few miles from Ft. Lauderdale to Hollywood a year later. I was able to get a job at the Winn Dixie Supermarket just across the street from the duplex where we now lived. I stocked shelves with a couple of other guys a few days a week. It was brainless work, but good exercise. Twice a week we unloaded huge trucks and lifted heavy boxes onto conveyor belts and then into storage units.

I worked the 5am-Noon shift on Saturdays and Sundays. At that time, I was unaware that lack of sleep was a trigger for seizures in epileptics. Only now do I know that some of the seizures I had while employed at the Supermarket were due to waking up early after going to sleep too late. Luckily, I never had a seizure while at work, but I still had seizures intermittently for several months.

Now, unable to drive, swallowing four pills a day that made my gums bleed and swell, I found myself almost hopeless and at the lowest point of my young life. We switched doctors and altered medications. Nothing seemed to work and every few months I would suffer yet another seizure.

Unbeknownst to me, my father was calling hospitals around the country to try to find a doctor that might be able to help me get control over my epilepsy and live life as a normal teenager. After calling the Mayo Clinic and countless hospitals, he found someone at Columbia Presbyterian in New York City. It's funny how just a simple phrase can trigger old memories. Whenever I catch that scene in *Airplane* where the captain is speaking to Doctor Hamm on one line, and the Mayo Clinic on the other, I am reminded of my father calling around desperately on my behalf. "Put Hamm on 5 and hold the Mayo."

My father was unhappy being retired and wanted to open up a store and return to selling furniture in New York again. That, coupled with his desire to find me a better neurologist, prompted our move back to New York. My parents vowed to find a doctor who would give me back my life. Somehow, with luck and God watching over us, they did just that.

When my parents shared the news with me I was elated. I would finally be near my friends again, and I would soon be allowed to resume driving since the six months the doctor suggested were almost up. Because we would be in an area with better access to public transportation, we decided to sell my Mustang and buy another car once we settled back into New York. Life was looking up.

A month or so before we moved, however, I suffered another seizure, and my doctor sent me to the hospital for further testing. This required a few overnights. I must have been in the pediatric wing, because after just an hour of settling into my room, another boy about my age was wheeled in and placed in the bed next to mine. The nurses came in and removed his clothes at a feverish pace and replaced them with a hospital gown. When he turned toward me, I was struck by his glassy eyes and the numerous cuts on his face. Soon after, his mother burst into the room and had to be calmed by the nurses. He had been taken from the scene of a car accident, and she came straight from work unaware of the seriousness of his condition.

The nurse told her that he was fine, except for a few scratches, but that he had to be tested for drugs, as he appeared to be under the influence of something. Those tests would be a mere formality. As they were moving his jeans to hang them up in the closet several pills fell out of his pocket and rolled onto the hospital floor. I picked one of them up and saw that it was stamped Rorer 714. I recognized it immediately as a kid in my English class always drew a giant version of the pill on the board when our teacher was late to class, which was basically every day. When I had asked him what it was, he told me it was a Quaalude. Drugs never interested me because my friends from Yonkers never took them and, because my doctors said that recreational drugs combined with my epilepsy could have disastrous consequences for me.

My classmate could not believe that I had never heard of Quaaludes. Drugs were much more prevalent in Ft. Lauderdale than in Yonkers back then and I learned that Quaaludes are a synthetic, barbiturate-like, central nervous system depressant. It's a sedative-hypnotic drug. Rorer was the name of the manufacturing company and the sale and use of Quaaludes by the students in my school was pervasive. They've since been discontinued.

It was hard to tell what kind of person was lying next to me in the room because he was so lethargic and spoke only in random fragmented sentences for the first few hours. Once the evening rolled around, however, and the drug wore off, he seemed to burst out of himself and wouldn't shut up. I didn't mind, however. He was a natural entertainer, a true raconteur. He had one of those "bad boy" personas like Matt Dillon in all those classic S.E. Hinton movies. He regaled me with hilarious stories of excessive drug use, sexual conquests, and more. I didn't believe half of what he said until the next day during visiting hours.

At least half a dozen beautiful teenage girls came to the room to visit him, ministering to him as if he were a rock star and they were his groupies. One was better looking than the next, and they each spoke to him as if they had been dating for years. I basked in his glory since they included me in their conversations and I found myself hoping the doctors would let me stay in the hospital a few more days just to absorb the atmosphere a little longer. I had never felt so close to stardom and would have been more than happy to have this guy's leftovers. I had no problem living my life through him. Of course, I wasn't so lucky, and was released early the next day.

CHAPTER 14

A TEACHER'S TEACHER

During my second and final year in Florida, I visited Alan back at Sadore Lane. We had a blast catching up. I also went back to Roosevelt High for a visit and Mr. Krell asked me speak in front of the band to tell them how music programs were run 1400 miles away. Mr. Krell wanted me to explain how competitive the band was in Florida. I told the students that in my new school you could challenge other musicians at any time if you wanted to move to a higher seat in the section. You also had to perform certain musical arrangements to earn your grade. Later on, a group of us recalled earlier days in junior high where Mr. Krell was also our band director. He was famous for his gastritis. If you were in his office and he thought you said something stupid, he leaned to the side and let one rip. This was known as the "one cheek sneak." He was the most animated teacher I ever had, and every concert was a lavish production with the best music teenagers could ever hope to play. His leadership as a band director was truly legendary.

While visiting the new band room in the high school, some students and I reminisced about my clarinet solo with the jazz band when I was in ninth grade. Eight hundred people were in the audience and I was doing a great job until Mr. Krell tried to raise the microphone. It slipped out of the stand and banged into my mouthpiece, driving it straight into my lip. A bloody mouth does not make for a great clarinet solo.

Our marching band was always excellent as well. We played in front of President Ford in White Plains, New York during his re-election campaign. We got in trouble because one of the songs we played was *Sweet Georgia Brown*. Mr. Krell hadn't realized that it was Jimmy Carter's theme song, President Ford's opponent at the time.

Twenty-five years later, the local paper would interview several students about teachers that had a major impact on their lives. They were asked to describe a teacher who had a profound influence on them. I felt fortunate and grateful that one of those students, Michelle Farber, cited me. Michelle's parents, Syd and Lenore were close friends of mine and her father was the principal of the school at the time. The newspaper did a follow-up story a few weeks later and asked all of the teachers named to recall their own favorite teachers. I named Mr. Krell. A week later I received a heartfelt thank you letter from him. I felt both honored and sad at the same time as I was reminded that the move to Florida deprived me of three years that should have been the best high school band experience.

Catching up and reminiscing with old friends was a great experience. It was also bittersweet as it reminded me that I no longer lived there; I missed my friends and would not graduate or attend the prom with them. I went to school with most of these kids for over 15 years. Now, I was basically a stranger in my new high school in Florida. I did not know at this time that we would be moving back to New York, but we'd all be out of high school by then.

I learned a very humbling lesson during that trip back home: life goes on. Although I now lived 1400 miles away, I knew that my adversity was just that, *my* adversity. I had loving parents who suffered as I suffered, and friends and family in two states who wanted the best for me, but it would be my decision how I would handle my obstacles. Attitude was everything. I could no longer live in the past and had to focus on moving forward, one day at a time.

CHAPTER 15

THE JAI LIFE

Something my father passed on to me was his love of gambling. When I was young, the house was crowded with his buddies on football Sundays, each one screaming over the other at the television set, alternately urging their teams on as they made their way down the field to score and cursing them when they failed. This is how I learned about point spreads and "covering."

I used to hear him on the phone with his bookie saying, "Give me the Jets 10 times." A "time" was equivalent to five dollars, so 10 times would be 50 bucks. My parents never had notepads in the kitchen and my father would write on anything in front of him. I was embarrassed once when I returned a report card to my fifth-grade teacher that had my mother's signature and, next to that, in my father's handwriting-*The Knicks five times!*

My father was an excellent bowler and was in a league that met each Sunday morning at Yonkers Bowl on Central Avenue. After bowling, he would come home with bagels and whitefish salad from Waldbaum's, which was right next to our apartment complex. Although my father's bowling leagues consisted of friends who made small bets during matches, there would always be heavy wagers made between a smaller group of them once the league time concluded. On many occasions, my father took a friend of mine and me along and we bowled in a nearby lane. It was always exciting because anytime someone got a turkey, three strikes in a row, everyone would scream "DIMES" and everyone would hand a dime to the bowler. If someone got a mark (a strike or spare in each of the 12 frames), they yelled "QUARTERS" indicating that everyone had to pay that bowler a quarter. My father won many dimes and quarters and passed them on to me so I could play video games while he continued to play for even higher stakes.

One of his friends from Sadore Lane joined the matches and brought his daughter along. Nadine was in my grade and we kissed a few times in the bowling locker room. The third time we were together there we pronounced ourselves married. We divorced during recess at P.S. 31 a few weeks later.

My father also hosted a monthly poker game that was more entertaining than any television show I ever watched. This would be the highlight of my month, since I was assigned to be the waiter for the first few hours. They usually started around 7:30 in the evening and went on until well past midnight. I would take orders for sandwiches and sodas and they would take a dollar out of the "kitty" for about 10 pots in a row, and that would be my tip for the night.

In the summer months, I would become a mobile waiter during his softball leagues as well. The men would order sandwiches and sodas and give me cash to run to the nearby deli and pick up their snack orders while they played ball. My father was once in the local newspaper that I delivered, *The Herald Statesman*, for hitting a home run in one of the games at the age of 55. The tips were great then as well. Unfortunately, a few weeks into the season, another father brought his son and we had to split orders, and that cut into my tips. Free enterprise sucks!

I was finally able to gamble legally in Florida when I turned 18 and I didn't lose any time doing so. The week of my 18th birthday I went with Larry, Jeffrey, and a few other friends to Dania Jai Alai, which, as it turns out, was less than five minutes away from Jaxson's Ice Cream Parlor. To me, Jai Alai was a glorified game of handball played with baskets. It was exciting to watch, but even more exciting was the fact that you could win money betting on the outcome of the matches. Because some of my friends were older than I, they had already been to Jai Alai and were well versed in the nuances of the game. They taught me about betting on matches and betting on long shots, which included trifectas where you had to predict the numbers of the top three winners. I said we should pool our money and bet on a 2-5-7 trifecta. They argued that a trifecta was impossible to hit, so we bet on the favorite, number 2, Juaristi, who actually came in first. Of course, 5 and 7 came in second and third respectively. It would have paid over $500 if we had bet! Almost 20 years later, I got even when I bet the 2-5-7 trifecta at the Meadowlands Racetrack in East Rutherford, New Jersey. It was my friend Lori's 50th birthday celebration and I chipped in with her husband, Phil. The trifecta hit and we split well over $1,200. Phil was able to cover the entire bar tab for the party!

Soon after my first experience at Jai Alai, my full reddish beard garnered me the name Burger King. I looked just like the guy who played the Burger King on the television commercials. I had just been accepted to the University of South Florida in Tampa, on a partial clarinet scholarship, and things were starting to seem a little more stable. I had enough credits to graduate six months early. Since I didn't like school much anyway, I had no reason to stick around and wait for my class. I asked Heidi out, my first Floridian girlfriend, and we went out for a number of weeks. Unfortunately, I lost my temper and broke up with her when she told me that her parents would not allow her to drive with me after she told them that I had epilepsy. They never even gave me the courtesy of asking me if I was controlled with medication or any of the particulars of the illness. It also didn't help that my friend, Jeff, dated her one night and made out with her in his car. Jeff's father was a really nice man and very funny as well. He found out about what happened and knew that I was upset with his son. He took us both into the living room and told us about a similar problem he had had with a friend when he was in high school. He made out with his best friend's girlfriend in the car but ran out of gas on the ride back from the date. He had to call his best friend to give him a lift home. He said he learned his lesson that friends are more important than girlfriends and that his son should learn the same thing. I told him that all I learned from the story is that the apple doesn't fall far from the tree and that both of them were assholes! We all laughed and Jeff apologized; we were fine after that.

Although I now understand why Heidi's parents didn't want me to drive her in my car, it was times like these that caused me to feel inferior and self-conscious about my condition. Shortly after that, my parents and I embarked on our return journey to the homeland. Not Israel. New York. It didn't make sense for me to remain in Florida since I would now have to pay out of state tuition for college as my parents would no longer be residents. My life would change for the better and, even though there would be difficult times in between, I realized that my illness didn't have to control me or who I was. My two years in Florida were not without positive experiences, but, for the most part, leaving Yonkers at the age of 16 and being diagnosed as an epileptic teenager was a most difficult time in my life.

I guess you could say, for someone who was accustomed to seeing people make crazy bets on everything from sure things to long shots, it frustrated me when people I came to know were unwilling to place a small bet on me. It hurt that they couldn't see the good kid beyond the condition with which I was afflicted, and which few of them ever witnessed. Not my father. He never gave up. In many ways, my father's gambler mentality allowed him to keep betting on the chance that he could find the right doctor and put me in the right situation to live a better life. He knew as well as anyone how hard I had it, battling against a condition few knew much about at the time. He hated losing more than he loved winning and he wasn't going to stop until he felt like he'd beaten the epilepsy. That mentality infused me with a sense of not wanting to lose either. A belief that I carry with me to this day and for which I have him to thank.

CHAPTER 16

AS GOOD AS GOLDENSOHN

My father tried to get us another apartment in Sadore Lane, but none were available and other Westchester County rentals were too expensive. We spent about two weeks in an efficiency hotel in Westchester and ventured over the Tappan Zee Bridge into Rockland County in search of a place to live.

While driving over the Tappan Zee one day, we noticed an appealing apartment complex overlooking the Hudson River. We exited and spent the next hour or so trying to find it. You could see it easily from the bridge, but it just seemed to disappear in the mist once we crossed over. We gave up on it, but ended up in Valley Cottage and found a condominium complex nestled behind the woods. Although most of the units were occupied by their owners, there was a rental agent who found us a nice two-bedroom. We moved in a week later. Soon after that, my father made an appointment with Dr. Eli Goldensohn, a well-known neurologist at Columbia Presbyterian. In one visit, this man changed my life forever.

When we first arrived at Columbia Presbyterian

Hospital, I was less than impressed. It did not seem modern or welcoming in any way, and Dr. Goldensohn shared a large space with several other doctors. The furniture was old and the room looked more like a bus depot than a physician's waiting room. We waited almost an hour until a balding man in his mid-sixties came out and introduced himself. We walked into his office and sat on the opposite side of his giant oak desk. He took out a small tape recorder and spoke into it as he asked us at least 50 questions relating to my epilepsy: the type of seizures I had, how I felt on certain medications, and other aspects of my illness. He called my seizures "episodes" and told me that some epileptics often experience myoclonic jerks. In epilepsy, myoclonic seizures usually cause abnormal movements on both sides of the body at the same time. They occur in a variety of epilepsy syndromes that have different characteristics. He focused on my illness, which he believed was juvenile myoclonic epilepsy. The seizures usually involve the neck, shoulders, and upper arms. In many patients the seizures most often occur soon after waking up. They usually begin around puberty or, sometimes, in early adulthood in people with a normal range of intelligence. In most cases, these seizures can be well controlled with medication but it must be continued throughout life. I still take the medication he prescribed that day 32 years later. He weaned me off of Dilantin and prescribed a medication that was relatively new in the U.S. Valproic Acid was not well known at that time, but Dr. Goldensohn said he thought it would be an excellent medication for me. He could not have been more correct in his diagnosis. Since the age of 19, I had not had a single grand mal seizure while on that medication. The medicine was also called Depakene, and because I had some stomach issues with it, he adjusted it to Depakote. A week after seeing Dr. Goldensohn I was watching the original *Hawaii-Five-O* in bed with my parents. This episode was most memorable to me because the guest star was an actor named William Smith.

Although many know Smith from his work in one of the Clint Eastwood *Every Which Way* movies, he was also one of the supporting leads in the television mini-series *Rich Man, Poor Man* starring Nick Nolte and Peter Strauss. To me, this was one of the greatest mini-series on television next to Alex Haley's *Roots*. Smith played Falconetti, nemesis to Nolte's Tom Jordache. He was built like a bodybuilder and had many memorable fight scenes with Nolte. While watching him on *Hawaii-Five-0* that night, I started to become incoherent. This petit mal seizure always preceded my grand mal seizure by about 15 to 30 minutes or even a few hours. For the first time since being diagnosed with epilepsy, I had a period of incoherency that was **not** followed by a grand mal seizure. I would never have a grand mal seizure again until we experimented with being medication free about 10 years later.

While being seizure free for a decade was an incredible accomplishment and nothing short of a miracle, I still had to living with the reality that a seizure could occur without warning. I would last for months without thinking about it, but then I would wake up in the morning and ask myself if having the illness was a dream. I would often say to Ivy, "I can't believe that I'm an epileptic." Taking medication was no longer a constant reminder of my disease and simply became part of my daily routine. Interestingly, I never thought about my sickness while I was teaching. I was always engrossed in my lesson and had to spend much of my time and energy on classroom management while dealing with difficult students. Whenever I made presentations in front of the faculty or in the summer as a camp administrator, that is when I had to think inward and check my brain for how I felt. Was I dizzy? Did I feel out of sorts? Even a bad night's sleep was cause for alarm if I did not feel "normal" when I woke up. Luckily, as the seizure-free years progressed, I was able to continue my life with fewer incidences of focusing on my adversity.

CHAPTER 17

MOVIE MAGIC

When we returned to New York in August of 1980, it was too late to apply to any four-year colleges so I decided to go to Rockland Community College (RCC) for a year or so until I was able to apply to a four-year school. Before I could register for classes, I had to take an entrance exam in English and Math. I knew I would bomb the math portion and ace the English. As expected, I bombed the math section, but I also tanked the English exam. I told them I was always an A-plus student in English, but they refused to retest me. After just three days in the remedial English class the teacher, Dr. Draper, said that there must have been a mistake because he thought I was an excellent writer and immediately switched me into the Honors Program. This was easy for him to do since he was in charge of that program.

Some of the other classes in the Honors Program were challenging, and I never felt as if I were getting a subpar education. I remember once forgetting to read the book assigned in my *Marriage and the Family* class and I based a paper on the book jacket and only the first 20 pages. I received an A-minus, but beneath the grade the professor wrote, "Marc, your writing is very strong, but this paper seems curiously repetitive." I was impressed by my increasing ability to work well quickly, but equally impressed that I wasn't able to sneak this past my professor.

A hard worker ever since my penny-saver delivery days, I soon found a job at the local movie theater in Nanuet. The Movies was a five-theater complex on the south end of the Nanuet Mall. On my first day the assistant manager, a young woman who seemed out of place in her position, introduced me to the other ushers. They all seemed friendly enough. Then she walked me over to a giant of a teenager, Andy, who had the nickname "Big A" because there were two other ushers named Andy; the short one was Little A, and the other one was Middle A. Big A was playing a video game and ignored the introduction. I thought to myself that the A in Big A probably stood for Asshole. So much for first impressions. In short order, Big A became one of my best friends, and still is to this day. He will be the first to admit, however, that he is an asshole.

My years at the multiplex theater were some of the best of my life. I was back in New York, seizure free, working, dating, and having the blast I should have had while I was in Florida. On most weekends, the ushers, cashiers, and candy counter workers went out to the Triangle Pub after we closed the theater. They had the best french fries that were served drenched in their signature gravy. Ah, to be young and calorie unconscious. The assistant manager, Jimmy Vazquez, who later became a close friend, was the first to invite me out after work. Jim, Big A, and I had a great friendship. We always laughed at Big A and his crazy antics. We used to prank the other ushers by filling up cups with ice and pouring them on their heads when they went to the bathroom for a "sit-down." When it was finally time to prank Big A, we dumped an extra-large popcorn tub full of crushed ice into the stall. We couldn't wait to see his reaction. To our chagrin, he emerged from the stall totally dry with his usher jacket accompanied by the umbrella he had opened while tending to his business. Big A - 1, Ushers - 0.

One time, we got worried when we did not hear from Big A after he missed his shift. But when a movie in one of the theaters ended, he walked out yawning after having taken a two-hour nap!

It's important to point out that Big A was the only usher to receive three raises in a single year without ever asking for one! Soon after we became close friends, he shared with me that he was blind in one eye. I had no idea. He was an excellent athlete and one of the most coordinated people I'd ever met. I confided in him that I was an epileptic and we both realized that all people, regardless of age, suffer from human frailties. He was a great baseball player and also attended RCC. He was told he would not be allowed to try out for the baseball team because of his "disability." The school felt that if he injured his "good" eye, they could be held liable. I was the editor of *The Outlook*, the RCC newspaper, and wrote a front-page article detailing Big A's frustration at not being able to try out for the team. After many students and teachers read the article, the coaches were told by the administration to give him a tryout. There were just 18 roster spots available, and he was awarded the final spot. We later learned that the coach left the final decision up to the team as to which of the two remaining players should be chosen to join the team. I was happy to be a part of his big ("A") victory.

No insult ever bothered Andy. One day, he burst into *The Outlook* office laughing hysterically and handed me a copy of the article I had written. He had found it in the men's room. Someone had cut one of his eyes out with a pencil. This would upset most people. The only problem Andy had was that he wished he had thought of it first.

After I told him about my epilepsy, he was very sympathetic and asked a few questions to make sure that if I ever had a seizure in front of him, he would be prepared. Several years after that, when I was married, he sent me a Christmas card. He knew I was Jewish and celebrated Hanukkah, but he couldn't resist. On the front of the card was a picture of Santa Claus twisted on the floor with his tongue falling out to the side and foam around his mouth. When I opened the card it read . . . SEIZURES GREETINGS!

I am not sure why I was now able to deal with my illness differently. Was it the natural maturation process? Was it being back in New York? Was it the medication? I like to think that it was because I had a support system in place and had educated myself about my illness. Increasing my knowledge increased my power to combat the negative aspects of my condition.

CHAPTER 18

THE BRINKS ROBBERY

I want to take a step back to recall the tragedy of October 20th, 1981. It has nothing to do with my condition, but it was a monumental experience in my life. I find it mind-boggling that I was only 19 years old, pretty much the age of my two sons today. Before I give you my account of what I witnessed on that fateful day, I would like to share an excerpt from Wikipedia that describes the infamous Brink's robbery.

"Car Swap: After fleeing the scene, the robbers drove to the parking lot where a yellow Honda and the U-Haul truck, manned by members of the May 19 Communist Organization, were waiting. The robbers quickly threw the bags of money into the car and truck and sped away. In a house across the street, an alert college student spotted them as they switched vehicles and called the police."

I am the college student mentioned in this excerpt; however, I was not so alert, and I didn't have the option of calling the police.

Several months before the robbery, I was driving down Mountain View Road on the way to Route 59. I was in my 11-year-old 1970 red Cutlass that I had recently purchased for $700. Another car swerved and ran into me. My front end was banged up, but all of the damage was at the bottom of the vehicle and the car was still drivable. The policeman on the scene filled out the accident report in my favor. The driver's insurance company paid me $700 and, since I never made the repairs, I was able to pocket all of the money. This accident and car played a major role in my experience with the police almost a year later, although the situation would of course be far more dangerous.

Andy Lennane, Big A, who several years later would become a correction officer at the Rockland County Jail, is also a participant in my memories of the occurrences of October 21st. He spent several minutes in the jail's elevator with Kathy Boudin, one of the masterminds of the robbery.

That morning Kathy Boudin dropped her infant son off at a babysitter. She then waited in a nearby parking lot as her accomplices drove a red van to the Nanuet Mall where the Brinks truck was making its pickup. That same day, I drove my red car around the county on some errands before I had to bring my dog, Pepper, to the Vet in Valley Cottage. One of my errands was to drop my mother off at the beauty parlor. This was a three-hour ordeal. I dropped her off and said I would be back later to pick her up. She reminded me that I was always late and that she didn't want to wait around all day for me to come get her. Her hair salon was **IN** the Nanuet Mall, **just one door down** from the bank that supplied the bags of money that were stolen from the Brinks guards later that afternoon. She was in the hair salon during the entire robbery and its aftermath. She later told me how lucky she felt that I was nowhere near the robbery when it took place. She, of course, had no idea how close I was to the worst part of it all.

When I arrived at the vet after dropping off my mother, the receptionist informed me that I had the wrong time, that the appointment was actually an hour later. I didn't feel like waiting there and didn't want to drive back home. I remembered the basketball I kept in the car so I went up to the condominium complex where I used to live to shoot some baskets. I tied Pepper to the pole and shot foul shots for about an hour. When it was time to return, I put Pepper in the passenger seat and headed toward the condominium exit and out onto Mountainview Road.

I am often amazed that I can't recall what I had for breakfast on any given day, but I remember the details of the next 30 minutes of my life as if it were yesterday. I still can't believe that these events took place well over three decades ago.

As I drove down the hill, a woman in a car was swerving and coming toward me. This seemed like déjà vu all over again. I figured she would hit my car and I would collect another $700. I thank God that her car did not hit mine. If it did, and her passengers got out of her vehicle, I highly doubt I would be alive today.

This was the car swap alluded to in the *Wikipedia* article. I thought I saw two kids wielding toy guns in the front and back seat, the driver screaming at them like they were misbehaving. These were not innocent kids, however, wielding toys. These were murderers brandishing their murder weapons in the face of an unsuspecting motorist whose car they had just commandeered at gunpoint.

I saw the car turn into a housing development as I made my way down Mountainview Road toward Route 59. As I looked to my left and passed the entrance to the Thruway, I saw a U-Haul and two police cars at the side of the road. I didn't think much of it until I realized that both patrol cars had their windows shot out. I crossed over Route 59, parked my car across the street, rolled down the windows for Pepper, and ran over to the patrol cars.

It was then that I witnessed the fatal injuries sustained by officer Edward O'Grady and Waverly Brown. I am no doctor, but I knew there was no way they would survive. When I turned around, two police cars became almost 10. The street was cordoned off, and a helicopter flew overhead. Policemen were crying and yelling and I heard one near me yelling into his walkie-talkie. Someone said that the suspects stole a car that matched the description of the one that almost hit me. I told the officer that I saw where the car was headed just two minutes ago. "We have a witness. We have a witness!" he screamed into his walkie-talkie. Before I knew what was happening, I was thrown into a patrol car with four other officers and soon we were speeding up Mountainview Road. I pointed to the area where the car had turned. They jumped out of the car and pulled shotguns out of the trunk as two other police cars pulled up alongside. The officers started kicking down doors of nearby houses and searched the area. I was left alone in the police car. In the deep recesses of my mind, I wondered what would happen if, due to the incredible stressful situation, I would experience a seizure.

Luckily, that did not happen. When I saw one of the suspects running into a wooded area, I shouted to one of the officers, and he ran after her and was able to tackle her before she got away. I was driven back down the hill as some of the suspects were apprehended.

When I got out of the police car, someone from the Journal News was on the scene and asked me what role I played in the recent events. I did not want to give my name, especially since some of the suspects were still at large.

When I finally drove to the Nanuet Mall to pick my mother up she told me I wouldn't believe it, but the bank next door to her hair salon was held up. I told her I knew that already, and proceeded to explain what happened to me shortly after the robbery.

When I told her of my involvement in the robbery escape, she cried for about 20 minutes. When we got home I called Nyack Hospital and asked about the condition of the police officers. I was surprised that they would talk to a stranger, but I was told that, unfortunately, both officers had "expired." That's the word they used. Expired.

The next day, I went to work in Manhattan with my father. We saw police vehicles with officers riding shotgun, and cars were being searched at the toll booths.

As the arrests continued to unfold, I brought up my experience that semester with my professor at RCC. I was taking a law class, and the Rockland County District Attorney at the time, Ken Gribetz, was my instructor. A few months later, he asked me for a written account of what I experienced that day. He asked if he could include some of what I described in a book he was writing about crime in Rockland County during his tenure as District Attorney.

I gave him permission, but asked that my name be left out, and he agreed.

Fast forward 20 years or so later, and Kathy Boudin and others were up for parole. I wrote an editorial about making sure we did not forget the atrocities that occurred on that October afternoon. Several people I didn't even know called me to say that they were happy that I wrote the editorial making sure we remembered what happened and who was responsible.

In 2017, I was asked to speak at the Brinks Memorial Scholarship Brunch. This is a ceremony where scholarships from the O'Grady-Brown Scholarship fund are given to local college students who are pursuing a career in law enforcement. I was the first witness to speak at this annual ceremony, and it was an emotional and gut-wrenching experience for me as the relatives of the police officers killed in 1981 listened as I retold my story.

CHAPTER 19

THE COLLEGE COLLAGE

A year or so after that, I left RCC to join Alan at SUNY Albany. Because I was starting as a junior, I was allowed to bring my car to school. My father was busy at work, and my mother didn't have a license, so I drove myself up to school. This was the first time I would be away from my parents for an extended period of time. Previous to this, our longest stretch apart was when I was 13 years old and attended sleep away camp for two weeks at French Woods Festival of the Performing Arts in upstate New York. I was part of the music program there. We did a production of *Oklahoma*, and I was playing clarinet in the pit. Unfortunately, I got sick the last few days of camp and never got to perform. It does, however, make me something of a six-degree separation to Maroon 5 and *The Voice* star Adam Levine. He attended the camp many years later, and supposedly met several of the Maroon 5 members there.

When I said goodbye to my mother the day I left for school, it was as if I were going off to war. A Jewish mother saying goodbye to her only son is not a pretty sight. She bawled and practically dragged herself to the car while grabbing at my body as I packed up to leave. My father took me aside and said, "You must promise me that while you are at school you will never snort marijuana or smoke cocaine." I looked him straight in the eye and swore on my grandmother's life that I would never snort marijuana or smoke cocaine. To this day, I have never met anyone who snorted marijuana or smoked cocaine. They must have made the same promise to their fathers.

My two years at SUNY Albany were some of the best years of my life. Although I only attended for two years, my stay there included meeting a cast of characters that have remained in the recesses of my mind to this day. Most people gravitate toward people that are similar to them when they go away to school, but I always loved meeting new and vastly different people. That is the main reason I never moved off campus. Not only did I love going down to the cafeteria and having my meals made for me, but also, it was like a hotel since so many other students were in the same hallway and building.

Alden Hall was an older residence hall at the downtown campus. Alan lived in Brubacher Hall, which was right next door. When I first arrived, I had to go to Brubacher to receive the keys to my dorm room. After my two-hour drive, I was about 30 seconds away from peeing in my pants when I finally found a bathroom. The place was packed with parents and students excited to begin their college experience. When I received my rooming assignment, I drove over to the next building and parked in one of the areas near Alden. I unpacked my car and started to make my bed when my new roommate, Paul, came in with his mother and father. Paul was from Queens and he had already been at Albany for two years.

Paul and I hit it off immediately. The only thing we didn't share was a taste in music. Paul was into groups I had never heard of, like Depeche Mode and Duran Duran. He was into new wave, as was everyone else in my age group. I was old fashioned, having been raised on Frank Sinatra, Steve Lawrence, The Barry Sisters, and the soundtrack to *The Man of La Mancha*. Paul was an excellent floor hockey player, and Albany had a really good intramural sports program. One of our other dorm residents, Grayson, was the goalie for the team, so many of us went to each game to support them. They won the championship that year, and it was very exciting.

Our first night together, I decided to tell Paul about my epilepsy. I was only controlled for about a year and a half and because he would be with me each night, I thought it was important that he knew the signs of a petit mal seizure in case it preceded a grand mal seizure. He was very understanding and shared with me that he often talked in his sleep. That night, around 2am, he jumped up and screamed at me, accusing me of stealing his camera. He almost gave me a heart attack as I was in a dead sleep at the time. We yelled at each for a few minutes until I realized he was not awake. Moreover, he didn't own a camera. We laughed about it the next day.

Paul was a talented artist and used his skills to sweet-talk many female students. He was very popular with the ladies, and enjoyed playing the field all year long. One night, he came back to the dorm with a girl who he really didn't like that much. Even though I was in the next bed, I was fast asleep, and she was practically falling all over him. After close to an hour of making out with her, he decided he'd had enough, but he didn't know how to get rid of her. He told her that he thought I was waking up and they should stop fooling around. This, of course, was not true, and she didn't want to leave. When she turned toward him and wasn't looking, he yanked my hair really hard to wake me up. She finally left the room, but so did a nice percentage of my hair! I believe he is responsible for my partial baldness today.

Back in the 1980s, colleges usually displayed a "ride board" that would list the names of people and where they traveled home during certain school breaks. This way, you could drive home with them if you lived near that area for about $5 a ride. Paul came up one day and told me that he had met a girl near the bus stop who said she was from Rockland County. He told her his roommate also lived in Rockland and that maybe she could get a ride home with me when school was over.

The next day, Ivy and her roommate, Peggy, came to our room to introduce themselves. I was not dating anyone at the time, and decided that since they were both from Rockland, I would try to see if I liked one of them enough to go out on a date. Being shallow, I was hoping they had either a doctor or a mechanic in the family. A doctor would mean I would possibly marry money, and a mechanic would be great since I had an old Cutlass at the time that needed constant repairs. I liked Ivy, but it absolutely sealed the deal when she told me that her father owned County Automatic Transmissions, a Rockland

County Transmission shop. I asked her out the next day and we have been together ever since. One of my friends, Eric Silver, always asked me how my relationship was going with "*My Yiddishe Momma.*" That was his nickname for Ivy and coincidentally, my father's favorite Jewish song. I told Eric after my first date that I would marry her.

Ivy and I were huge professional wrestling fans. One year in particular, Captain Lou Albano and Cyndi Lauper were teamed up for wrestling entertainment, and Ivy and I decided to dress up as the duo for Halloween. She dyed her hair red and I wore a safety pin and rubber band on my cheek. Today, we are married 28 years and together over 30.

After Ivy and I were dating for several months, I abandoned the Cutlass and bought a different used car. Her father was thrilled that I would be able to drive her back to Albany after one of the breaks. We had just finished packing the car when I put it in reverse to back out of their driveway in Chestnut Ridge. For some reason, the car must have been dyslexic because even though I threw it in reverse, it decided to go forward. We had to unpack the car and load her dad's car, and he had to drive to Albany after all. This is the second time I pissed him off.

The first time occurred when we met in Albany. Ivy's parents had come to visit her and invited me to join them for dinner at the Publyk House Restaurant in Vermont. Ivy's mother was always a stylish dresser and she came into the dorm room wearing a black cape. Alan happened to be there. Since that day he's referred to her as the dragon lady. When we got to the restaurant, there was a bit of a wait. Ivy's father and I were eating peanuts from a dish on the mantle. I kept pulling the dish toward me and he kept pulling it toward him. The last time he tried to get peanuts he put his hands in the nearby ashtray by mistake. Boy was he surprised by the taste of cigarette butt and ash. He thought I did it on purpose, but I swear by the hair left on my head it was an accident.

When my parents came to Albany to visit me, I took them on a tour of the campus. They wanted to meet Ivy, and I said that she was studying in the library and we could go there to see her. I was not exactly the most serious student. I looked around the campus until my father finally realized that I didn't know where the library was located.

I told my parents that Ivy knew I had epilepsy, but I still had some anxiety about them bringing that up when we were all together for the first time. It didn't help that my grades were less than stellar. Since my parents' financial status changed drastically, I paid for college myself. Between grants, student loans, and money I received from various jobs, I put myself through college. I was actually very proud of that. If I flunked out of school, it was my money and my responsibility.

It was very important to me that my parents and Ivy got along. I was pretty sure early in our relationship that Ivy and I would get married. We had a very nice visit, and they liked her very much. My father was happy that she was so studious and hoped that her habits would rub-off on me. Well, at least he could hope.

CHAPTER 20

THE GOLD RUSH

While attending SUNY Albany, I joined the college newspaper. Although I wrote a few stories, I soon found out that selling ad space was a paid position. I already had a job at night making calls for the college fund, but I wanted something else in order to finance my dates with Ivy. It's not that I was a great boyfriend, but Albany had some of the worst college food in the country. We called the hamburger nights Murder Burgers. I had worked for the UA food services in the cafeteria, but my mother begged me to quit after I bleached the floor incorrectly and was almost asphyxiated. I put the bleach in the bucket before the water. It seems that you are supposed to do it the other way around in order to avoid noxious fumes. That's when I decided to try selling ad space.

I sold to local restaurants and eventually made a deal with someone who owned a clothing shop. His father also had a connection for knockoff fragrances. I sold his merchandise on the campus at the small fountain in front of the student union. Word spread that I was making good money for him, which led to my being hired to sell 14K gold jewelry for his friend as well. She did really well, and when I told my father I could do the same thing if he were my partner, he fronted me several thousand dollars to invest in gold jewelry. As it turned out, the gold dealer my client used was just minutes away from my home in Rockland. When I left Albany, I went into the home show jewelry business for a year or so. During that time, I saw an ad in the local paper for a summer job as a counselor and van driver for a local day camp. I had been a counselor before, and although I was doing fairly well in the jewelry business, I decided to apply for the job.

The camp was a franchise with a smiley face as its logo. This particular one was owned and operated by Steve and his wife, Lois, who later became close friends. Steve asked me many questions at my interview, but to this day, we still speak about two specific questions. First, he asked if I planned to wear my gold chain during sports activities. This is the same necklace I wear presently. My parents bought it for me as a present because we moved so abruptly to Florida when I was 16. It is almost 30 grams and, as the saying goes, "they don't make 'em like that anymore." He then asked what I would do if "little Tommy" sat on the side during volleyball. I told him I would ask Tommy if he didn't like volleyball or if he felt he wasn't good enough to play. Then I told him I would play Newcomb ball with Tommy as a lead-up game to improve his confidence. He liked that answer, and the rest is history. In my present-day camp consulting business, I use the same role-play questions when training day camp and residential camp staff both in the Tristate area and Canada.

I have often heard that youth is wasted on the young. While this is true, it is also true that when you are young, you don't have the pressures of monthly bills and exorbitant credit card charges. Some people would say that I was broke while in college; however, $5 and a ten-cent chicken wing special made me feel like a millionaire. This is part of the innocence of youth.

Being away at college, however, spared me the harsh reality that my parents were struggling financially. To this day, I do not know if we had proper health coverage. I have no memory of purchasing my medication. My father was working for a car service, and I only know that their lifestyle had changed drastically at that time. I suspect that if I were not seizure free during that time period, it would have resulted in a catastrophic financial hardship. I wish I had been there to help them, but I was playing the role of college teenager wrapped up in his own life. They never shared their money troubles with me verbally, but deep down I knew.

CHAPTER 21

FIRST CLASS

You either love my friend Steve or you don't. While some people mistake his straight from the hip responses as arrogance, I can only say that I hope my own sons find a friend as loyal as he is when they are grown. Steve was always a mentor to me, and he called me immediately when his friend and principal, Marvin Budow, said that he needed more teachers at his school. Steve was a guidance counselor at The Angelo Patri School, and he thought I would be a natural at teaching. I was doing well with the jewelry business, but I did not have any health benefits. This was in 1985, and New York City teachers had just got a whopping raise. New teachers made $18,500 a year plus benefits with summers off! What could be better?

I interviewed with Mr. Budow and was hired immediately as a seventh grade English teacher. I like to think I gave a good interview, but many said that I simply passed the New York City Teacher Mirror Test. Some claimed that if the principal put a mirror in front of you and you could fog it up by breathing, you were hired.

I went down to the Board of Education in Brooklyn,

signed a contract where I promised I would earn 12 more education credits within a year, and started work in the Bronx just a few weeks later. My first day, I went to use the bathroom and knocked on the locked men's room door. It was occupied at the time, not surprisingly, by Steve. While most normal people would say, "Just a minute," or "Occupied," Steve simply screamed out, "Go away!" Arrogant you say? I fell over laughing. Arrogance is in the eyes of the beholder.

One of the department heads put chalk in my hand that day and said, "Good Luck. Just try to keep them seated."

Thus began and ended my formal teacher training. My first-period class was an NIEH class—Neurologically Intellectually Emotionally Handicapped. I have terrible handwriting, and when I wrote on the board, not only was it sloppy, it slanted uphill and grew larger with each word.

"You don't have to write *that* big! We're not *that* retarded!" someone said. I turned around to find Felipe laughing hysterically in his chair. Then I glanced out the window and noticed that there were bars covering the glass. To this day I am not sure if the bars were there to keep intruders out, or keep the teachers in. This was the beginning of a difficult yet most rewarding eight-year training exercise which taught me how to manage a classroom. It astounds me that this memory seems like it happened yesterday. Felipe is now 43 years old!

My parents loved Steve. Although strongly opinionated, he was usually right, and they were happy I had someone who could advise me. I told him about my epilepsy, and he asked me many questions that others never thought to ask. I wanted him to know since we would be working in the same school and carpooling together. It was at this time that Dr. Goldensohn asked if I wanted to experiment with going off of my medication. He thought that this was the time to try. He also said that the Depakote stayed in your system for a while and I would still be protected. He added that if I were seizure free for 18 months, I was most likely safe forever. Sixteen months later I suffered my worst seizure ever. The medication was completely out of my system by then and I was totally unprotected.

The day after I was observed by one of the assistant principals, she called me into her office for my post-observation conference and gave me a glowing report. She said that I was a natural, that the kids loved me and she loved the lesson. I was excited and couldn't wait to tell Steve. I went to his office but was told he had just left for a meeting. I walked back to the elevator and when the door opened for me to walk in, two other staff members stepped out. I could not remember where I was or where I was going. They stared at me and I stared back at them. They said hello but I did not respond. That is the last thing I remember before a powerful grand mal seizure wreaked havoc on my body.

I must have walked about 50 feet into a nearby hallway. At that point, I had the seizure. A teacher found me on the floor. I had fallen hard and was bleeding heavily from my mouth. I chipped a tooth and bit into my tongue. Nobody knew what was going on. Security thought that I might have been stabbed. They put the school on lockdown while I was taken away by ambulance. My friends and colleagues, Bernice and Joan, went with me to St. Barnabus Hospital in the Bronx. I think the seizure was more pleasant than the hospital.

My first memory is opening my eyes in one of the Emergency Room beds and seeing Bernice looking over me. She was visibly shaken and walked away. This happened several more times. I later learned that I had at least six seizures in the hospital bed. It was too much for Bernice to witness. As I slowly came out of the grogginess, I was taken for tests. There was a stab wound victim next to me in the hallway. When Ivy finally arrived with her mother, the person who was stabbed moaned incessantly. We didn't know where to run first. Steve found out what happened and came immediately to the hospital. I was released just a few hours later and Steve drove us to the school and my parked car. Ivy's mother drove us back to Rockland, and, as groggy as I was, I felt a rush of memories returning to my frazzled brain. This was the same car ride that I remembered while being driven home after my seizure in the motel near Disney World. Dr. Goldensohn was upset when I called him the next day and told him about the seizure. He received the reports from St. Barnabus a few days later and called me immediately. He said that the seizures were intense and that it seemed that instead of the few hours of incoherency or petit mal activity that I usually experienced, this time the smaller seizure lasted only a few brief moments. He attributed that directly to the lack of medicine in my blood system.

Over the years, I had been tested regularly to make sure that the medication did not adversely affect my liver. Since my tests always came back negative, he suggested that I stay on the medicine. I was always in the therapeutic range of blood levels that were between 50 and 100. Experimenting with being taken off the medicine was worth a try once, but not again. He also said that my amino acids were totally out of whack due to the seizures, and that I shouldn't exercise for several weeks. Additionally, he did not want me to drive for several months until the medicine was built up in my system and blood tests showed that my level of protection was over 50 percent. Ivy had to drive me to the carpool every day, and I was unable to drive Steve or Bernice for almost three months. What took 12 seizure-free years to accomplish was undone in a single day. I experienced the same car ride home I had in Florida as a young teen, and I needed to once again count on others to drive me everywhere. Once more, it was déjà vu all over again.

During the seizure in school, I bit my tongue so badly that after I had the chipped tooth fixed, I needed to go to a specialist who gave me medication for my tongue. I was in intense pain for a few weeks until it finally healed.

I was not sure how I would handle the questions and comments when I returned to school. Well-wishers asked how I was feeling, but even as an adult, I was anxious about discussing the seizure.

People didn't know what happened and I told those that inquired that I had a bad allergic reaction to a medication I was taking. Only Steve, Bernice, and Joan had any idea what had really happened. I often joked with Steve that the one day I actually needed him he wasn't in school. He made up for it though. Two years later, I broke up a fight between a substitute and a student and the student threw a table at the substitute that hit me by accident, breaking my foot. Steve drove me to my doctor in Rockland while avoiding as many bumps in the road as possible as I screamed in pain. I spent five weeks at home watching Luke and Laura's torrid love affair on *General Hospital*. I was on crutches for more than a month before I was allowed to return to school.

When I began my career as a middle school teacher in the Bronx, I was given large manila record card packets for each student in my homeroom class. These record packets contained everything from family information and former report cards to medical history. It shocked me that so many students had asthma listed as a medical condition. Several of the students suffered from epilepsy and even had the medications they were taking listed. Almost all of those with seizure disorders were on Dilantin. I tried not to look at these students differently, but I would sometimes find myself searching them during class for possible signs of seizure activity. Many epileptics don't have petit mal seizures preceding a grand mal seizure. I am an anomaly compared to most other epileptics in that I never had a grand mal seizure unless it was preceded by a petit mal seizure.

This is my greatest regret. Instead of telling people the truth, I hid my infirmities and treated them as if I should be ashamed. I was afraid people would not look at me as they use to and they certainly wouldn't treat me the same way. I was seizure free on the medication, but I was afraid people wouldn't want me to drive them anywhere. Would the school allow me to chaperone a trip alone? When you are in your twenties, you are supposed to be indestructible. I saw my illness as a weakness, and I now realize that is a slap in the face to all those with any kind of disability. My only excuse was my youth and inexperience. I could have related so much better to students who I saw suffering each day. Some had parents who were addicted to drugs, and others lived in poverty. Young teens were living every day battling far worse conditions than I had ever experienced. If I only knew then what I know now---I have said that to myself many times over the years. So much time wasted while I selfishly hosted my own pity party. I could have been a better teacher, friend, and person. This is why I decided to put pen to paper and continue to tell my story.

CHAPTER 22

JULIUS SEIZURE
AND THE SINS OF THE FATHER

For about three years, I taught tenth grade English. In one of the scenes from *Julius Caesar*, Cassius is angry that Caesar is gaining favor with the people of Rome. Most people are not aware that Caesar was an epileptic. Many years ago they described people with epilepsy as having "the falling sickness." Since most people fall down during a seizure, the name was certainly appropriate. In this scene, Cassius says the following:

"And this is the man who has now become a god, and I'm a wretched creature who must bow down if Caesar so much as carelessly nods my way. In Spain, Caesar had a fever, and it made him shake. It's true, this so-called "god"—he shook. His cowardly lips turned white, and the same eye whose gaze terrifies the world lost its gleam. I heard him groan—yes, I did—and the same tongue that ordered the Romans to obey him and transcribe his speeches in their books cried, "Give me some water, Titinius," like a sick girl. It astounds me that such a weak

man could beat the whole world and carry the trophy of victory alone."

This always reminded me of my fear that certain people would see my illness as a weakness. Nevertheless, my fears and priorities changed as time went on.

Luckily, Ivy and I never thought much about the possibility of passing my illness on to our children. Since my doctor said it usually skipped a generation, I chose to focus on the present, not the future. Ivy and I were determined to live our lives to the fullest and raise our family with the hopes for the brightest of futures.

Several years and two children later, my eldest son, Craig, was diagnosed with ADD. Although I am still uncertain that this was an accurate diagnosis, he had an excellent pediatric neurologist. There are many in the medical field who do not recognize ADD/ADHD as a medical diagnosis. Dr. Goldensohn had retired and my neurologist in Rockland County, Dr. Earl Zeitlin recommended Dr. Sherbany for Craig. I first met Dr. Zeitlin when he was on the Youth Group Committee at Monsey Jewish Center where I was the youth director. He is a great musician, amazing man, and well-respected physician. I trusted his recommendation and knew that Craig was in great hands with Dr. Sherbany. Many people say that I am a little ADD myself. I was quite relieved when Dr. Sherbany said that the country would not run without people who had ADD. A few years ago when I was on an antibiotic, I went upstairs to take my pill. Later on, while tutoring someone for the SAT, my student said that he couldn't believe how slow and clear my instruction was that day. I found out several hours later that I took

Craig's ADD medicine by mistake. When Craig and I are together it is often a battle of wills: ADD vs. DADD.

The next summer, Craig went to sleepaway camp. Someone I worked with when I was a Youth Director in Rockland County, Jerry Marcus and his wife Enid, owned the sleepaway camp. It was there that Craig met Zack, one of his best friends. We brought our younger son Scott to see Craig on visiting day during the third week of camp.

Camp Lindenmere is located about 90 minutes from our house in Henryville, Pennsylvania. We had just returned from visiting day when the caller ID showed a call from the camp. Ivy answered the phone and was visibly shaken. She handed it to me and the camp nurse said that Craig had what she thought was a seizure. I said we would be there as soon as possible to take him to the doctor. I called Dr. Sherbany and he said to bring Craig to the hospital where he would be doing his rounds later that evening. I went into our hall bathroom, buried my head in a towel and cried. I asked myself if this was to be the legacy given to my first-born son. I was crying almost uncontrollably. As quickly as I started, I stopped. As difficult as my epilepsy was for me, I know that it made me a better and stronger person, and I knew that whatever ailment Craig had would be dealt with as a family. He was exactly the same age as I was when I was found unconscious in the laundry room. We were told that his new camp friend, Zack, spent a lot of time with him in the infirmary until we arrived. It was comforting to know he wasn't alone while he waited for us to arrive.

I had always thought epilepsy was supposed to skip a generation, and just assumed my boys would be spared.

Perhaps I was wrong. When Dr. Goldensohn was still practicing, we called him when Craig was an infant. Craig was not sitting up by himself and this concerned us because I read that people who were on Depakote sometimes had children who had spine problems that caused problems with sitting. Dr. Goldensohn assured me that this was exceptionally rare, and impossible in this case because the issue had been found only in women who took the medication and not men. Craig sat up just fine two weeks later.

When I came out of the bathroom my eyes were beet red and Ivy could see that I had been crying. She didn't mention it then and she hasn't mentioned it since. That night, Dr. Sherbany saw Craig and determined that he had heat stroke. It has now been almost 10 years and there have been no further episodes. The focus has now shifted away from my illness to a new priority—the health and welfare of my children.

I have decided that my illness does not define me; I shall define it. Almost 20 years after my mother's passing, I was diagnosed with Diabetes Type 2. I was never overweight and always followed a reasonable diet. I take this as a gift from my mother. I have a very good doctor, recommended by Steve Mayer, of course, and I went to a wonderful Nutritionist, Sharon Saka, also from Rockland County. I know many diabetics and often see them in the doctor's office during my visits. Many of them are overweight and eat as if they do not have diabetes. They have let their disease rule them, and not the other way around. I hired a personal trainer and embarked on a physical journey that has changed my life and those in my family as well.

One of my students told me about a boxing class she went to just a minute away from our school. Steve and Eva Eckert, owners of Peak Physique Bootcamp and Boxing, offer free boxing every Thursday evening. I attended the class and after a while, Ivy did as well. We liked Steve so much that we hired him as our personal trainer, and we went to boxing class almost every week. Craig and Scott have attended training, too, and Craig shed over 30 pounds three years ago. Mental and physical health is tremendously important for a person's well-being and we do whatever we can to protect ourselves against illness.

CHAPTER 23

THE TEACHER
BECOMES THE STUDENT

Now, almost 40 years after my first seizure, I find myself at the end of a teaching career where I teach more than 100 students a day. I own a tutoring service that offers in-person and online classes. I present workshops on Camp Staff Training, Classroom Management, SAT and ACT Prep, and a host of other topics. I have been the emcee at over 10 retirement parties making jokes at the expense of others, and even composing and singing songs that celebrate people's careers in education. I have presented seminars in front of hundreds of people, none of whom know that before I begin my presentation, I know that there is a chance, however small, that I could have a seizure in their presence. After staying up late at night on cruises or other vacations, I am always attuned to how I am feeling and listen to my body to make sure there is no absence or incoherence in my brain.

While doing camp consulting work at Camps 'R' Us in Long Island a few years ago, I was visiting with the owner, Gary Turnier and his son, Jason. Gary was actually the founding member of Gary's Gang, a disco group in the '70s whose most notable hit was *Keep on Dancing*. Gary was the lead drummer and tells the greatest stories about the music business. His passion for life and camping has been handed down to his son and, together, they run several camps in Long Island.

Gary was telling me the story of how he was signed to a label in the early '70s. In the middle of the story, my mind went blank, and I seemed to hear the story in slow motion. I tried my best to refocus but was having great difficulty. I was almost certain that I was going to have my first seizure in 22 years. I said I had to go to the car for a minute, breathed in deeply, and tried to calm myself down. I had a protein bar in the car and thought that perhaps my sugar was low. Low sugar is not part of the problem I have as a Type 2 diabetic, but I was trying whatever I could do to shake the feeling of falling into the state of a petit mal seizure. A few minutes later, I felt better. I don't know what caused that lack of focus, but I would not experience it again until a few years later.

More recently, my youngest son, Scott, was diagnosed with Irritable Bowel Syndrome (IBS). The Hobermans don't have the best stomachs, nor do we have the best genes. It has been troublesome to him and caused him to fall into states of depression. He was almost 17 and on the verge of college. It brought me back to my own difficult teen years. It was then that I decided to finish this book, which I had started many years earlier. Unless you are a parent, it is hard to imagine the emotional toll a child's illness can have on you. The frustration and helplessness is almost too much to bear. You truly wish the pain could be transferred to you. I never saw my parents visibly worried when I was sick, but I now know how helpless they felt. Ivy was very upset about Scott's condition and kept asking me how I was able to remain so calm.

I finally realized that it was my experience with epilepsy as a teen that made me stronger instead of weaker, healthier instead of sicker. I know that I am more focused and in partnership with my own mind and body at all times. Most importantly, I have faith in God and myself that we can handle whatever is put before us, especially if we have the support of family and friends in times of need. I also spoke with Scott and told him that, like my parents, his mother and I would leave no stone unturned in finding help for him. After visits with several doctors he is finally beginning to feel better, is exercising again, and eating as if he were sentenced to the electric chair.

I have become the man that I am today not in spite of my illness, but because of it. It is easy to be happy and move forward when things are going well, but much more difficult to advance when things seem to be in a downward spiral. The thoughts my mother shared with me when I was first diagnosed with epilepsy resonate vividly today. The most important thing is to define your troubles and learn from them. Don't ever let your struggles define you; you define you.

Chapter 24

HISTORY REPEATS ITSELF

In the summer of 2016, I was tutoring a student for the New York State English Regents. I was taking an antibiotic for bronchitis and was also prescribed a medication for a rash. The doctors believe that the combination of the medications lowered the efficacy of my Depakote. The result of my experience that day was that I had to add a chapter to my memoir. My story was not yet finished.

While tutoring, I became unable to recognize the words in the passage I was reading. I began to ramble a bit, but somehow managed to complete the lesson. I went upstairs and told Ivy I did not feel well and was going to cancel my remaining lessons scheduled for that day. Then I said something I was never able to articulate before: "This feels just like a seizure." I texted the students and told them I was not feeling well and that we would have to reschedule. At least that's the message I thought I sent. The message they received was vastly different. from the one I intended. What I actually wrote was sdlfkdkasfadsfheoikjelk,nn,mdnfdfndplkd. The preceding sentence is not a typo. It is the message I typed even though my brain thought I wrote something completely different.

Ivy and Scott were afraid that I might be having a stroke. Scott proceeded to ask me to smile, stick out my tongue, and raise my hands. I was able to comply without any problems, but Ivy decided to drive me to the hospital just in case. I became increasingly incoherent in the car, and was speaking gibberish by the time we arrived at the emergency room at Good Samaritan Hospital.

After several tests, the neurologist told me that it appeared that I had a petit mal seizure. He also said that even though I was controlled on Depakote for well over 30 years, newer drugs were on the market, and I should switch to another medication called Keppra. I told him that I needed two hours to make up my mind.

When he left the room, I cried for the entire time. I felt myself going back in time to when I was first diagnosed with epilepsy as a teen. My head was spinning. How could I possibly stop taking a medication that had protected me for over three decades allowing me to keep my illness a secret? Now, however, things were different. I refused to fall into a two-year depression yet again. Two hours was all I needed. My struggle would not define me; I would define myself. When the doctor returned I said, "Thanks for waiting. Let's start the new medication." I knew there would be side effects and obstacles along the way, but I took things one day at a time and am once again seizure free.

EPILOGUE

In the past year, I have been a guest on over 35 radio shows including WCBS NY 880AM and was voted as one of their Top 50 Human Interest Stories of 2017. I have spoken at countless high schools and colleges and continue to help students, parents, and educators overcome adversity. I donated a class set of books to the PMM School in Jinja, Uganda, and was able to have a book discussion via Skype with Chole Richard's amazing group of young students. I have written a study guide for the memoir which has been used in several high school classrooms and have also created a radio show called Lighting the Educational Flame. I'm just getting started.

As time moves forward, I am comforted by the fact that I have shown my children that although there are often tremendous obstacles in life, when the front door is locked, you have to try another door. If necessary, break a window. I hope that others who experience struggles gain strength from reading about the search for my true self. The self I defined by declaring a major part of my life as *Adversity Defeated* by recognizing that my adversity was an *Opportunity in Disguise*.

ABOUT THE AUTHOR

Marc Hoberman is an educational consultant, best-selling author, and motivational speaker.

He wrote *Opportunity in Disguise: How I Defeated Adversity* as a way of exposing the advantages he has gained as a result of a difficult situation. He would not be the same person had he not encountered these challenges.

Marc founded Grade Success Education in 1995 and has since expanded his tutoring company to include online tutoring, educational videos, and courses nationally. From the boardroom to the classroom, Marc continues his passion to help people of all ages reach their full potential.

Social Media:
www.facebook.com/gradesuccess
www.instagram.com/grade_success
twitter.com/GradeSuccess

Websites:
www.marchoberman.com
www.gradesuccess.com

Available for Speaking Engagements, School Visits
Contact marc@marchoberman.com

Additional Materials:
Opportunity in Disguise Study Guide

Order additional copies from:
LeRue Press, LLC
280 Greg Street, Suite 10
Reno, NV 89502
www.Lrpnv.com
Bulk purchases and school discounts available.